AMERICAN CHURCH

RUSSELL SHAW

AMERICAN CHURCH

*The Remarkable Rise, Meteoric Fall,
and Uncertain Future of
Catholicism in America*

Foreword by
Archbishop Charles J. Chaput, O.F.M.Cap.

IGNATIUS PRESS   SAN FRANCISCO

Cover Image: The oculus of the dome of the Basilica of the National
Shrine of the Assumption in Baltimore Maryland. The Basilica was
designed by Benjamin Henry Latrobe between 1806 and 1821. Latrobe
was America's first professionally trained architect, and Thomas
Jefferson's architect of the US Capitol.:

Cover design by Milo Persic

© 2013 by Ignatius Press, San Francisco
All rights reserved
ISBN 978-1-58617-757-7
Library of Congress Control Number 2012942824
Printed in the United States of America ⊗

CONTENTS

FOREWORD:
YOU SHALL BE MY WITNESSES

There's a passage in Acts that I've reread and reflected on ever since I was a young priest: "And you shall be my witnesses in Jerusalem and in all Judea and Samaria and to the end of the earth" (Acts 1:8). I go back to that verse again and again, because it reminds me that the believing community that began in Jerusalem's Upper Room now preaches Jesus Christ around the world. And that always renews my hope. In the wake of ten difficult years for the Church in the United States at the start of the twenty-first century—in fact, as Russell Shaw so eloquently details in these pages, it's been a difficult half century—we need to remember that over the centuries, God has always called men and women to renew and extend his Church. Today that same vocation belongs equally to every faithful Catholic.

The apostles who preached the gospel on the first Pentecost had several things in common. Each had been called by Jesus. Each had known him firsthand. Each had denied, failed, and abandoned him. Each had repented. Each had been forgiven. And each, despite his sins, had received the same commission: "Go therefore and make disciples of all nations" (Mt 28:19). Jesus knew—in advance—the sins of every man he chose. And still he chose them, and still he sent them out to convert the world in his name.

Therein lies the mystery of every Christian life. God sanctifies the world with sinful clay. The clergy misconduct scandal of the early 2000s is a tragedy in every sense. But it is not unique. From the Old Testament to the present day, the story of God's priests and God's people has been one of sin, chastisement, repentance, conversion, and renewal.

The problems we face today as believers really aren't so different from the ones we've faced in the past. God calls us to spread the light of Christ despite the shadow of our own sins. This is the paradox of all discipleship. It's God's school of humility. We're not worthy to be disciples, but God calls us to that work anyway. In bearing our sins with humility, our weakness becomes the antidote to our pride, and this enables us better to serve God's will. Scripture teaches us that when Israel had worldly success, she failed. So it is too with the Church. What we need to learn from our failures as a people of faith is our own inadequacy without God.

There may have been a time when a genuinely Catholic life could be comfortable or placid. But if it ever *really* existed, that time is over.

The men and women God calls today, and the people the Church needs today, must be heroes. Striving for heroism needs to be part of our daily lives. We need to be people who love God more than ourselves; who seek God's glory more than our own; who want to lead by serving others; who have a mercy and a humility born of a knowledge of our own sins; who have the courage to preach the truth even in the face of contempt; and who have a hunger for winning souls. We need to be people who are faithful to the Church and her teachings and who witness the joy of Jesus Christ to others.

The world we live in is not a friend of the gospel, no matter how superficially "religious" American culture may still sometimes seem. It has contempt for Jesus Christ, contempt for the Cross, and contempt for the people who carry their own cross and follow him. In the years ahead, the kind of people we need are believers who will turn away from comfort, who will listen for the voice of God, who will follow Jesus Christ into the storm and, in their failures, turn to him as Peter did: "So Peter got out of the boat and walked on the water and came to Jesus; but when he saw the wind, he was afraid, and beginning to sink he cried out, 'Lord, save me.' Jesus immediately reached out his hand and caught him, saying to him, 'O man of little faith, why did you doubt?'" (Mt 14:29–31). This is the kind of faith that changed the world from Jerusalem to all the ends of the earth. And it's really the only kind of faith that can change the world of today.

To put it another way, we teach other people with the example of our lives. If we believe, others will more readily believe. If we are holy, others will more easily hear their own call to holiness. The "crisis" in today's Church is finally a crisis not of resources but of baptism; it is a crisis of faith. The central issue of modern American Catholic life is the temptation to accommodate, to compromise, to get along, and to fit in—and then feel good about it. We accept tepidness in the name of pluralism. We put diversity of belief and behavior above truth. We place the individual above the common good. We elevate "tolerance" above love, justice, and real charity. None of this converts anybody. It does the opposite. It provides people with alibis for indifference and inaction, and it leeches away their faith.

It's important for us as disciples to fully understand the culture of our time—from the economic pressures dividing families, to the power of the mass media, to the appeals of consumer comfort, to the persuasiveness of science and technology—without being captured by it ourselves. We can't give to others what we don't have ourselves. If our own faith and zeal and desire for souls are weak, we can't expect anything different from the people around us.

What people really believe, they act on. And when they don't act, they don't really believe. For all of us as American Catholics, this issue of faith is the heart of the matter. Real faith changes us. It hammers us into a new and different shape. We too often confuse faith with theology or ethics or pious practice or compassionate feelings, all of which are important—vitally important. But real faith forces us to face the deeply unsettling command given to each of us in the First Letter of Peter: "As he who called you is holy, be holy yourselves in all your conduct" (1:15).

Holiness means being in the world but not of it. It means being *different from* and *other than* the ways of our time and place, and being conformed to the ways of God, as Isaiah says: "For my thoughts are not your thoughts, neither are your ways my ways, says the Lord. For as the heavens are higher than the earth, so are my ways higher than your ways, and my thoughts than your thoughts" (Is 55:8, 9).

To the degree Catholics have longed to join the mainstream of American life, to become like everyone else, to accommodate and grow comfortable and assimilate, rather than be "other than" and holy, we've abandoned who we really are. Clergy and religious face this temptation just as vividly as laypersons. Like the Jews in the days of Jeremiah, too many American Catholics have too often forgotten the covenant. We've "burned incense to other gods, and worshiped the works of [our] own hands" (Jer 1:16). We've ignored the final command Christ gave to all of us when he said, "Go therefore and make disciples of all nations." He was speaking to each of us, right here and right now. Catholics are a *missionary* people led and served by a *missionary* priesthood.

So I think this, then, is the lesson of the last fifty years for all of us. We need to return to Christ's call to "repent, and believe in the gospel" (Mk 1:15). We need a Church rooted in holiness. We need parishes on fire with faith. And we will get them only when we ourselves fundamentally change; when we center our lives in God; when we seek to become holy ourselves.

Throughout his long ministry, Blessed Pope John Paul II urged Catholics again and again to take up the task of a "new evangelization" of the world. Seeking an armistice with the spirit of the world, both outside us and within us, is an illusion. The Church in the United States faces an absolutely new and absolutely real kind of mission territory every day now, filled with intractable pastoral challenges. We're a nation of wealth, sophisticated media, and excellent universities. We're also a nation of aborted children, the unemployed, migrant workers, undocumented immigrants, the homeless, and the poor.

We live in a nation of great material success and scientific self-assurance but also a nation where the inner life is withering away, where private spiritualities replace communities of real faith, and where loneliness is now the daily routine of millions of people.

America is mission territory—whether we recognize it yet or not; whether we live in New York or Atlanta or Phoenix—and we need a new Pentecost. We need to be people who are men and women of prayer, people of courage, people of service, men and women anchored in the sacramental life of the Church.

We need to be disciples who can answer generously and honestly *yes* when Jesus asks us, "Simon, son of John, *do you love me?*" (Jn 21:16, 17, italics added).

God is calling us to be those persons right now. He's calling us to the sainthood that he placed as a seed in our hearts when he formed us in the womb. And so the prayer we need to keep on our lips, as we look back on the American Catholic experience and look ahead to the hopes and difficulties that lie ahead, is "Thank you"—*Thank you, God*, for delivering me from myself; *Thank you, God*, for calling me to your service; *Thank you, God*, for demanding from me a life of holiness; *Thank you, God*, for giving me the brothers and sisters in faith to support me on the way. "And you shall be my witnesses in Jerusalem, and in all Judea and Samaria, and to the end of the earth."

Russell Shaw has lived his own life of Christian witness with uncommon integrity, humility, and keen intelligence. His skill animates every page of *The Gibbons Legacy*. He has captured the story of the Church in the United States with honesty and love, and it's a privilege to call him my friend.

+Charles J. Chaput, O.F.M.Cap.
Archbishop of Philadelphia
May 2012

ACKNOWLEDGMENTS

It will be obvious that *The Gibbons Legacy* is not a history of the Catholic Church in the United States. Rather, it is an attempt to sketch the process by which American Catholics have been assimilated into American culture during the past two centuries and to assess the impact cultural assimilation has had on Catholicism in the United States. I highlight only some major events and personalities along the way; readers looking for a fuller picture of what is described here should consult the works cited throughout the book.

Sections of *The Gibbons Legacy* have appeared in a different form in *America*, *Catholic World Report*, and *Crisis* magazines; in *Our Sunday Visitor* newsweekly; and on the Inside Catholic (now *Crisis*) website. I am grateful to the editors involved.

I thank several friendly critics who have done me the kindness of reading and commenting on some or all of the book. They are Dr. J. Brian Benestad; Prof. Gerard V. Bradley; Dr. Matthew Bunson; Dr. Jude P. Dougherty and members of the Old Docs dinner-and-discussion group; Dr. Lee Edwards; Dr. Germain Grisez; and Dr. Joseph Varacalli. Each has made a valuable contribution to the project. In the end, of course, responsibility for the book's weaknesses and deficiencies is the author's, not theirs.

I thank my daughter, Dr. Elizabeth C. Shaw, for her crucial technical assistance. A philosopher by training, she also possesses exceptional computer skills and commendable patience with those not similarly blessed.

Finally, I wish to extend special thanks to Archbishop Charles J. Chaput, O.F.M.Cap., of Philadelphia for his remarkable generosity in taking time from a crowded schedule to write a thoughtful foreword. I am honored to have his name associated with the book.

INTRODUCTION

For a long time the telling of the story of the Catholic Church in the United States has usually sounded something like this:

> Thanks to the fructifying grace of God, the grain of mustard seed ... has grown to be a large tree, spreading its branches over the length and breadth of our fair land. Where only one bishop was found in the beginning of this century, there now are seventy-five serving as many dioceses and vicariates. For their great progress under God and the fostering care of the Holy See we are indebted in no small degree to the civil liberty we enjoy in our enlightened republic. ... I proclaim, with a deep sense of pride and gratitude ... that I belong to a country where the civil government holds over us the aegis of its protection without interfering in the legitimate exercise of our sublime mission as ministers of the Gospel of Jesus Christ.[1]

It was March 25, 1887, when James Cardinal Gibbons of Baltimore spoke those words in Rome, in a homily that

[1] James Cardinal Gibbons, homily on taking possession of his titular church in Rome, Santa Maria in Trastevere, March 25, 1887, in John Tracy Ellis, ed., *Documents of American Catholic History* (Milwaukee: Bruce, 1962), 458. The growth in the number of bishops and dioceses celebrated by Gibbons has continued since then. As of 2012, there were 454 active and retired Catholic bishops in the United States and Virgin Islands, and 195 archdioceses and dioceses along with one apostolic and one personal ordinariate. The Catholic population of the country was 77.7 million and made up 22% of the total population.

accompanied his taking possession of the titular church assigned to him as a cardinal, the venerable Santa Maria in Trastevere. Pronounced in the backyard of the Vatican, the homily's praise of American ways and the advantages they offered to the Church were judged to be a bold stroke by the cautious Gibbons at a time when Americanist sentiments were regarded coolly by high-ranking personages in the Holy See.[2]

This praise of America and Americanism is central to the Gibbons Legacy.

Since 1887, Gibbons' words have been repeatedly quoted, cited with approval, and received as conventional wisdom in accounts of American Catholicism. Now the time has come to ask whether conventional wisdom gets the story right. Perhaps its version of events was correct back in Gibbons' day, but today American Catholicism finds itself enmeshed in a grave crisis that includes falling numbers of priests and religious; sharply declining attendance at weekly Mass and participation in the sacramental life of the Church; and a massive, continuing exodus by people, especially young people, who've lost interest in Catholicism, even as many others remain Catholic in little but name. At our peril as a Church we ignore the fact that this bad news, and much more besides, is related at least in part to the cultural assimilation of American Catholics into the American secular mainstream that was so enthusiastically promoted by Gibbons and others in his day and is still promoted by many within the Church even now. Much of this book is devoted to illustrating what happened in the past and how it goes on happening now.

---

[2] See John Tracy Ellis, *The Life of James Cardinal Gibbons, Archbishop of Baltimore, 1834–1921* (Milwaukee: Bruce, 1952), 1:309–10.

Yes, America has been good to the Catholic Church in many ways. As Cardinal Gibbons pointed out on that memorable occasion in Trastevere, American-style separation of church and state, long regarded with suspicion by Rome, preserved the Church from the sort of political entanglements that so often proved to be her undoing in Europe while helping to discourage the rise of the virulent anticlericalism that still exists in many parts of the Old World. Citizen participation in democratic processes has helped stimulate the participatory approach to church governance widely accepted as desirable—at least in principle—by the Church in America. And American egalitarianism has served as a natural basis for ecclesial *communio*.

Yet each of these positive elements of the relationship has its negative mirror image. Separation of church and state, in the hands of secularist ideologues, is a club for driving religion out of the public square. The ideal of participatory governance encouraged the excesses of lay trusteeism in the past and now fuels demands for a radical democratization of the Church. Egalitarianism in the ecclesial context easily becomes congregationalism. All these aberrations can currently be seen at work in American Catholicism. But what is happening now also is something new: we are witnessing a rapid institutional and numerical decline of the Church herself amounting to a kind of ecclesiastical implosion.

Even in the boom times of the nineteenth century, foresighted observers could see the stage being set for these developments. The best known of these observers was Orestes Brownson, the most distinguished (and very nearly only) American Catholic public intellectual of his day. In a letter of 1870 to Isaac Hecker, founder of the Paulist order and a former colleague with whom Brownson now profoundly disagreed, he wrote in part:

Instead of regarding the Church as having advantages here which she has nowhere else, I think she has here a more subtle and powerful enemy to combat than in any of the old monarchical nations of the world. . . .

Catholics as well as others imbibe the spirit of the country, imbibe from infancy the spirit of independence, freedom from all restraint, unbounded license. So far are we from converting the country, we cannot hold our own. . . .

I have hitherto wished to effect a harmony of the American & the Catholic idea, but I believe such harmony impracticable except by sacrificing the Catholic idea to the National.[3]

Brownson was ignored. The views of Cardinal Gibbons and other Americanizers—like Archbishop John Ireland of Saint Paul; Archbishop John J. Keane, first rector of the Catholic University of America; and Bishop John Lancaster Spalding of Peoria—prevailed. Generation after generation, Catholic newcomers (and their children and grandchildren)—Irish, Germans, Poles, Italians, and the rest—were more or less successfully assimilated into American Catholicism and, via the medium of the Church, into the mainstream of the larger American culture. Monsignor John Tracy Ellis declares the Catholic Church to have been "one of the most effective agencies in turning this vast army of foreign-born into law-abiding citizens whose children in the second and third generations gave witness of how thoroughly American they were".[4]

Although her success as an agent of assimilation was for a long time one of the Church's proudest boasts, there

---

[3] Orestes Brownson to Isaac Hecker, August 25, 1870, in *The Brownson-Hecker Correspondence*, ed. Joseph F. Gower and Richard M. Leliaert (Notre Dame, Ind.: University of Notre Dame Press, 1979), 291–92.

[4] John Tracy Ellis, *American Catholicism*, rev. 2nd ed. (Chicago: University of Chicago Press, 1969), 52.

were occasional stumbles. The Americanist crisis of the late nineteenth century was the most painfully visible. The judgment pronounced in 1899 by Pope Leo XIII in *Testem benevolentiae* that "those opinions cannot be approved by us, the sum total of which some indicate by the name of Americanism" was a blow to the Americanizers; but they quickly shook it off and denied holding the views that the pope had condemned. Since then, the substance of Pope Leo's critique of Americanism has frequently been ignored, and sometimes misrepresented, in accounts of this crucial episode. But the views rejected by the pope included not just (as is commonly said) the idea that American-style separation of church and state supplied a model for adoption by the Church everywhere, but also a subjective, individualistic approach to Church doctrine and discipline widely present among American Catholics now and justified by the supposedly direct, personal inspiration of each believer by the Holy Spirit. (These matters are discussed in chapter 1.)

The furor over Americanization notwithstanding, the process of Americanizing Catholics rolled on. For a long time that made sense. How far it carried Catholics can be seen in *The Cardinal*, a now generally forgotten but once wildly popular novel by Catholic author Henry Morton Robinson loosely based on the career of Francis Cardinal Spellman of New York.

A best seller from the very start, *The Cardinal* was published in 1950—early in the Cold War, that is, which also was the high-water mark of American Catholicism up to that time as measured by the intensity of Catholics' identification with the Church and Catholicism's impact on American society. At the heart of Robinson's novel is an ancient question: Can someone be a good Catholic and also

a good American? His answer, universally applauded by his
fellow Catholics, was a resounding, reassuring yes.

But *The Cardinal* went even further than that. Not only
could Catholics be good Americans, but by divine providence (so Robinson strongly implied) it is their God-given
destiny to be the very best Americans of all. As tensions
rose between the United States and the Soviet Union,
Robinson's prescription for saving Western democracy from
the menace of godless Red totalitarianism called for a de
facto alliance between America and the Catholic Church:
the United States would provide the money and military
might, while the Church supplied brains and vision.[5] Here
was Catholic triumphalism on a heroic scale.

As is now clear, *The Cardinal* made its appearance on the
brink of a historical precipice that shortly was to interrupt
the triumphant journey of American Catholicism toward
the glorious fulfillment foreseen by Robinson. Beginning
in the mid-1950s and continuing through the sixties and
seventies, the old subculture that nourished what sociolo-
gists call the "plausibility structure" of Catholic beliefs as it
was embedded in a vast network of institutions, organizations, and programs came undone under the impact of social
and demographic change (higher education for a growing
number of American Catholics, rapidly rising socioeco-
nomic status, suburbanization). Eventually the subculture and
its institutional framework were either dismantled or radically altered in line with policy choices advocated by Catholic intellectuals and academics and in due course approved,

---

[5] At a critical point in the story, wrestling with the question of the place
of Catholicism in the United States and whether a Catholic could be a good
American, the novel's hero Stephen Fermoyle finds his answer in Cardinal
Gibbons' 1887 homily at Santa Maria in Trastevere, quoted above. See Henry
Morton Robinson, *The Cardinal* (New York: Simon and Schuster, 1950), 293.

or at least accepted, by Church leaders. Hastening the death of the old subculture were currents of religious change flowing tumultuously in Catholic life during and after the Second Vatican Council (1962–1965), especially the post-Council agenda of engagement with "the world". In the twinkling of an eye, the Church in America, says historian Charles Morris, was "shorn of the cultural supports that had been the source of its strength".[6]

As this was happening, the secular culture into which Catholics were rushing to assimilate was itself experiencing radical change. Despite an ugly and deeply rooted vein of anti-Catholicism, American secular culture for well over a century and a half had provided a receptive and largely benign environment for the Church, just as Cardinal Gibbons and his friends insisted in the face of Roman skepticism. Now, in the 1960s and 1970s, cultural-revolution-*cum*-sexual-revolution changed that. In place of the old anti-Catholicism, the revolution in morality that the birth control pill helped usher in became the great new foe of the Church, undermining her mystique in the eyes of many of her own adherents.

How do things stand now? Let another cardinal answer that. Calling what remains of the original Protestant ethos of America "a secularized echo of Calvinism", Francis Cardinal George, O.M.I., of Chicago, a past president of the U.S. Conference of Catholic Bishops, underlines the consequences this holds for American Catholicism. "While the Church in the United States enjoys a certain institutional freedom," he says, "she exists in a culture that, in often surprising ways, resists Catholicism."

---

[6] Charles R. Morris, *American Catholic: The Saints and Sinners Who Built America's Most Powerful Church* (New York: Times Books, 1997), vii.

Culturally assimilated American Catholics who no longer
belong to subcultures that buttressed Catholic identity while
permitting interaction with society in general now have to
discover and foster in American culture itself the resources
they need to express their faith. If these resources are only
ambiguously there, American Catholics who have remained
somewhat distant from the dominant culture naturally hes-
itate over their relationship to it.[7]

And of course, rather than hesitating over their relationship with a secular culture in tension with their faith, very
large numbers of American Catholics plunge uncondition-
ally into that culture, at enormous cost to their identity as
Catholics.

At the start of chapter 4, I present several pages of dreary
figures that amply document the alarming declines in American Catholic participation in numerous areas of Catholic
life, from attendance at Mass to attendance at parochial
schools, during the last several decades. Without repeating
everything that's said there, I merely call attention here to
the results of a recent, comprehensive study of Catholic attitudes. The researchers asked whether it's possible to be a
"good Catholic" without observing various elements of
Church teaching and discipline. Among the 19% of the
respondents who considered themselves "committed Catholics", 49% said it wasn't necessary for a good Catholic to
attend Sunday Mass every week; 60% said that good Catholics didn't have to follow Church teaching on birth control,
46% the teaching on divorce and remarriage, 31% the teaching on abortion, and 48% the requirement of being married

[7] Francis George, O.M.I., *The Difference God Makes: A Catholic Vision of
Faith, Communion, and Culture* (New York: Crossroad, 2009), 85, 28, 34. Car-
dinal George is one of the comparatively few Catholic leaders in the United
States to have grasped this situation and written systematically about it.

in the Church; and 39% said that good Catholics needn't contribute time or money to help the poor.

Reading this, a friend commented, "It seems to me that there is an undeniable and severe crisis by any measure, at least so long as one thinks of Catholicism as something to believe in and adhere to because it is true. But so many Catholics today are universalists who think one religion is better than another only on subjective grounds of taste, biography, tribal loyalty, etc."

How we reached this point is the story *The Gibbons Legacy* tells.

"But", someone will object, "your story doesn't apply only to American Catholicism or to Christianity in the United States. In fact, the story is called secularization, and the secularization process is taking place everywhere in today's world and especially in the West, raising challenges to religious faith wherever it occurs." [8]

The observation is certainly true, but it also misses the point. To say American Catholics now live in a secularized environment is to say little more than that they live when and where they do. This statement of fact becomes the

---

[8] A word is in order here about the different meanings of several similar words. "Secular" refers to the sphere of life that lies outside the specifically religious sphere; as used here, and otherwise unspecified, it is a neutral term, with no prejudgment of good or bad implied. "Secularization" refers to the process by which progressively more of human life and experience go on in the secular sphere, and progressively less in the religious. It too is an essentially neutral term, with both good and bad results. The secularization of Western culture has been under way for the last half millennium or more. See Charles Taylor, *A Secular Age* (Cambridge, Mass.: Harvard University Press, 2007). "Secularist" and "secularistic", as used here, are negative terms referring respectively to individuals and a general state or condition more or less marked by hostility to religion and more or less committed to the suppression of public expression of religious belief.

statement of a normative analysis open to suggestions for modification only when it is specified in reference to particular cultural instantiations of the process that it describes: politics, higher education, the theological enterprise, and so on. That work of specification is something else *The Gibbons Legacy* proposes to do. Even when they are "reputed to have the same religions" as Europeans, George Santayana once remarked, Americans are "curiously different" from their European coreligionists;[9] in what follows, that difference is taken for granted in respect to American Catholics. It is the distinctiveness of Catholicism here, not its resemblance to Catholicism somewhere else—which includes a susceptibility to secularism—that provides the point of departure for this book.

I don't dream about some nonexistent golden age in bygone times against which today's Catholicism should be measured. The faith of the Catholic Church does establish certain definite parameters, but within those parameters many legitimate variations are possible, and many of these have probably not yet appeared on history's stage. Taking the Newman of *An Essay on the Development of Christian Doctrine* as a model in the recognition of continuity and change as complementary principles of ecclesial life, I seek as a Catholic to remain open to both and to avoid what Charles Taylor calls "premature closure" in matters of the spirit.[10]

Having laid out my argument and my illustrations in the first three chapters of this book, in chapter 4 I offer some suggestions about where American Catholicism needs to go

[9] George Santayana, *Character and Opinion in the United States* (London: Constable, 1924), 124.

[10] Taylor, *Secular Age*, 769.

next. Two ideas stand out: the need for a new Catholic subculture with a supporting plausibility structure, and the need to ensure that this subculture and plausibility (which are already beginning to take shape) are strongly oriented to evangelization—the "new" evangelization of which Blessed Pope John Paul II and Pope Benedict XVI have often spoken. Neither thing, subculture or evangelization, will succeed without the other.

Reviewing a book by Father Charles Curran of Southern Methodist University on "Catholics' movement out of their own subculture into the U.S. mainstream", Notre Dame theologian Michael Baxter writes: "For Curran, as for many of his generation, the story of Catholics entering the U.S. mainstream is a success story. There is little sense of a downside.... To pursue these concerns may seem to him like a step into the past, into the subculture we thankfully left behind. But it may also be a step into the future, into a form of the church that we cannot fully imagine." [11] Except for the fact, which he neglects to mention, that those "challenges" of identity and mission face not only Catholic institutions in the United States but millions of individual Catholics, Baxter is right. Readers of this book are invited to trace the trajectory of the intra-Church debate on these matters from the middle years of the nineteenth century up to the present day—and beyond.

The stakes in this particular argument are very high. German Catholicism in the 1930s provides an illustration. When Hitler came to power in 1933, some German Catholics were horrified, some took a nervous wait-and-see attitude, and

[11] Michael Baxter, "Curran Charts Catholic Move to the Mainstream", *National Catholic Reporter*, April 15, 2011. The book Baxter is reviewing is Father Curran's *The Social Mission of the U.S. Catholic Church: A Theological Perspective* (Washington: Georgetown University Press, 2011).

some were well pleased. In March of that year, the Catholic philosopher Dietrich von Hildebrand, seeing his homeland in the grip of a man he called the Antichrist, fled the country. While visiting Paris the following month, he was invited to lunch by the attaché at the German embassy. His fellow guests were the provincial of the Dominican order in Germany and the prior of the Dominican monastery in Berlin. "At table", von Hildebrand reports, "there arose a very disagreeable discussion."

> The provincial began by saying, "But we have no reason at all to reject Hitler when he stresses the idea of authority and the value of the nation. Above all, he keeps speaking about God." I answered, "Hitler is so stupid that he does not even know what the word 'God' means." ... The provincial continued, "We Catholics have to put ourselves at the front ranks of National Socialism and in this way give everything a Catholic turn." I answered, "National Socialism and Christianity are absolutely incompatible, and besides, it is a terrible illusion to think that Catholics would be able to influence this movement by means of compromises." ...
> After dinner the prior even began laughingly to sing the *Horst Wessel* song.[12]

What tune, one wonders, was the prior singing ten years later as Götterdämmerung drew near?

America today is a far cry from National Socialist Germany in 1933. God willing, that will always be the case. But it would be foolish and shortsighted to suppose the German experience has no lessons for the Church in other

[12] This passage comes from unpublished wartime memoirs of von Hildebrand. It is published here through the courtesy of the Dietrich von Hildebrand Legacy Project and its founder and president, John Henry Crosby, who also translated it.

countries, including the United States. How compatible with the values of the Catholic tradition, after all, are the values of secular America that so many assimilated Catholics more or less uncritically accept? Yes, Catholics have a serious obligation to be good citizens; but alongside good citizenship—in fact, arguably an important part of it—is the obligation to be critical of nationalism and the attitudes and behavioral aberrations to which it gives rise.

Catholics absorbed into the ethos of today's American secular culture feel very at home there. On the evidence, many appear neither ready nor willing to provide a Christian critique of things like legalized abortion, a nuclear deterrence policy about which the public knows (and apparently cares) little or nothing, the contraceptionist-consumerist mentality that dominates the American dream of material success, the idol of American exceptionalism abroad, and much else in the world view of contemporary secular America in serious tension with their religious tradition.

Finally, a word about the title of this book, *The Gibbons Legacy*, and about Cardinal Gibbons himself. James Gibbons (1834–1921) was a conscientious churchman who exercised an enormous influence on American Catholicism during a long and fruitful career. Relatively reserved by comparison with the flamboyant Ireland, less intellectual than Keane and Spalding, Gibbons by his patient, prudent diplomacy did more than anyone else to shape the Church in America in his day—and, arguably, in ours. I do not see him as either hero or villain but as what he was—a towering figure in the story of the Americanization of American Catholicism. As we shall see, he may also have something important to tell us about the future. If he does, that too will be part of the Gibbons Legacy.

I

EVERYBODY'S CARDINAL'S DREAM

For me more than for most kids growing up American Catholic in the 1940s, the cardinal's presence was a tangible, everyday fact. There he sat, after all, weathered a grayish green, a robed figure six feet high atop a pink granite base, every inch a prince of the Church. Southward he gazed from his throne, his expression grave yet mild, clasping the cross of Christ with his left hand and his right hand slightly raised as if aiming a blessing down Sixteenth Street at the White House and his great friend Teddy Roosevelt.

The inscription on the southern face of the monument's base reads:

JAMES
CARDINAL
GIBBONS
MDCCCXXXIV
MCMXXI

And on the north:

EMITTE SPIRITUM TUUM
ERECTED BY
THE KNIGHTS
OF COLUMBUS
MCMXXXII

Emitte spiritum tuum—Send forth your spirit: episcopal motto of Cardinal Gibbons, archbishop of Baltimore from 1877 until his death in 1921.

Perhaps it was the Spirit who, during those often tumultuous and conflicted decades, moved him to imprint a distinctively American character on the Catholic Church in the United States. Whatever the explanation, I call the Americanization of American Catholicism—the cardinal's greatest achievement—the Gibbons Legacy.

His statue stands in the Mount Pleasant section of Washington, D.C., dominating a small, triangular park at the intersection of Sixteenth and Park Road in front of a domed Byzantine church called the Shrine of the Sacred Heart. Modeled on the cathedral of Ravenna, the church is distinctive for its exterior of white concrete infused with fragmented quartz and the extensive mosaics inside. Here every Sunday, for more than twenty years, I shared in—or at least was present at (in a manner not unlike the cardinal's statuesque presence outside)—the celebration of the Eucharist in its pre–Vatican II form. Here too as an altar boy (altar servers were boys or men back then) I served hundreds of Masses and attended the priest at countless benediction services.

Going into the church and heading home afterward, I couldn't help but be aware of the statue presiding with silent dignity over its scruffy little park. I had no idea why Cardinal Gibbons was there. You could take it on faith he'd been someone important who'd done important things, but what important things he'd done I neither knew nor cared. Like the devout souls—mostly women and always including my mother—who turned out for everything at church, the cardinal was simply *there*: a presence without personal history of any known sort. Had I been a reader of Scripture, I might have applied to him the words of Hebrews about that mysterious Old Testament figure Melchizedek: "without father or mother or genealogy, [having] neither beginning of days nor end of life" (Heb 7:3).[1] As matters stood, I could only suppose, in the manner of children who naturally suppose all things that happened before they were born to have occurred in an equally and immeasurably distant past, that Cardinal Gibbons had been there in the park, rain and shine, since time immemorial.

Of course that was wildly wrong. The Gibbons statue had been dedicated just a few years before, on the afternoon of Sunday, August 14, 1932. Four years earlier, a joint resolution of the Seventieth Congress, introduced by Senator Millard E. Tydings of Maryland and Representative Frederick N. Zihlman, also a Maryland man, authorized its presence on public land. The statue was executed by Leo Lentelli, a Bologna-born sculptor and naturalized American, whose work today can be viewed not only in front of my old church but in such splendid settings as Rockefeller Center, the San Francisco Museum of Art, and the Breakers in Palm Beach, Florida.

In approving putting this memorial on public land, the congressional enactment declared it to be "a gift to the people of the United States" from the Knights of Columbus. Having laid out $36,000 to pay for their gift—a significant sum in those days—the Knights naturally turned out in force for the dedication, so that, according to the printed "Order of Exercises" preserved in the museum of the organization's New Haven headquarters, the event was preceded by a "Parade of Supreme Officers and Directors and Members . . . with other societies, military organizations and bands".

---

[1] All Scripture quotations are from the Revised Standard Version, Catholic Edition.

After an invocation by Pope Pius XI's apostolic delegate to the United States, Archbishop Pietro Fumasoni-Biondi, the Gibbons statue was presented by the Supreme Knight of the Knights of Columbus, Martin H. Carmody of Grand Rapids, and was formally accepted on behalf of the nation by no less than the president of the United States, the Honorable Herbert Hoover. In his remarks, the president said he'd come to know the cardinal during World War I and praised him for "carrying into the minds of other people the feeling that the truths of religion are really the primary aids in solving the perplexities of every day living."[2] No small praise coming from a man then wrestling with the perplexities of the Great Depression.

The unveiling of the statue was performed by Miss Margaret Gibbons Burke of New Orleans, a grandniece of the late cardinal, and was followed by a "discourse" by a bishop and a blessing by the apostolic delegate that brought the elegant and decorous proceedings to a suitably pious close. It's safe to suppose a good and edifying time was had by all, with the possible exception of poor Hoover, facing the prospect of crushing defeat in the November election.

As years passed and the statue took on its handsome green patina, the cardinal and his little park were noticed less and less. Mount Pleasant fell into decline, and what in 1932 had been a neighborhood notable for embassies, large churches, well-tended parks, upscale apartment buildings, and comfortable private homes on the perimeter of Rock Creek Park acquired a reputation for violent crime and drugs.

Mount Pleasant hit rock bottom in 1968, after the murder of Dr. Martin Luther King Jr., when rioting and looting erupted in the commercial stretch of Fourteenth Street

---

[2] Quoted in Ellis, *Gibbons*, 2:648.

a mere two blocks east of Sacred Heart. The fires that followed left block after block of gutted buildings in their wake, along with armed National Guardsmen patrolling the streets of the nation's capital. Since then, the neighborhood has made a slow but real comeback, so that today the Gibbons statue is in the heart of a lively multicultural section of the city, where African Americans, whites, and Latinos mix and mingle and it's as easy to buy a taco as a half smoke and chicken wings.

Despite the relative neglect that followed the 1932 dedication, once a year for many years the statue did receive significant attention. Every Labor Day a special Mass was celebrated in the Shrine of the Sacred Heart, with luminaries of the Church and the labor movement (many of them Catholics) in attendance. After Mass the important guests would stroll across the street to the little park for a wreath laying and speeches at Cardinal Gibbons' feet.

Growing up, I was dimly aware of these ceremonies, which were notable events in the calendar of the local archdiocese, although it remained a mystery to me why anyone would choose Labor Day to lay a wreath in honor of a cardinal. I didn't know that the yearly ritual recalled and celebrated a central episode in Gibbons' long and illustrious career—his successful defense of the Knights of Labor to the pope.

America's first big workers' organization, the Knights of Labor, was founded in 1869. Untrammeled capitalism was in the saddle at the time, and the very idea of an organized labor movement was anathema to powerful interests. In 1879, a Catholic, Terence V. Powderly of Scranton, was elected head of the group, whose members included many Catholics.

Alas, the Holy See viewed the Knights with suspicion as a secret society. The Church's European experience with secret societies like the Masons was not a happy one, and Pope Leo XIII's condemnation forbidding Catholics to join the Knights of Labor was thought to be imminent. At this crucial juncture Cardinal Gibbons, from a working-class background himself, spoke up publicly and also in private in defense of the Knights. His efforts climaxed in February 1887 in a memorial to Rome on the labor movement in general and the Knights of Labor in particular. It was imperative, he wrote, for the Church to be organized labor's friend, not its enemy. The cardinal prevailed. The Knights of Labor went uncondemned by Leo XIII. Many consider this Gibbons' finest hour.

The Knights of Labor soon faded, but the labor movement remained and prospered. The cardinal's intervention at a critical moment was remembered and appreciated as a brave and farsighted step sealing the bond between America's Catholic workingmen and their Church. Along with Cardinal Manning of Westminster, moreover, Gibbons of Baltimore was credited with having helped shape the pro-labor thinking, advanced for its time, that was soon to be a major theme in Pope Leo's historic 1891 social encyclical, *Rerum novarum*.

"Of all the many distinguished services which Cardinal Gibbons rendered to his Church and his country the championship of the Knights of Labor won for him the most enduring fame and the most grateful remembrance", says his biographer, Monsignor John Tracy Ellis.[3] And so, on Labor Day for many years, special Masses were celebrated in Sacred Heart and wreaths were placed at the foot of the statue across the street.

Many things have changed since Monsignor Ellis' monumental biography of Gibbons was published in 1952. Gradually, the luminaries of the Church and Big Labor who

---

[3] John Tracy Ellis, *The Life of James Cardinal Gibbons, Archbishop of Baltimore, 1834–1921* (Milwaukee: Bruce, 1952), 1:544.

attended the annual Labor Day rites became somewhat less luminous than their predecessors had been at the start. Fewer and fewer people took note of the whole affair. Today, the Archdiocese of Washington doesn't list a Labor Day Mass and wreath laying on its website calendar, and searching the site turns up no mention of any such ceremony in at least the last ten years.

People who are fond of symbolism will find it here. As the Labor Day Mass and the wreath laying are faded memories today, so also the special relationship between organized labor and the Catholic Church has faded and become largely an episode in history. For reasons that should become apparent in the course of this book, this also is part of the Gibbons Legacy.

My intention in what follows is to examine the Americanization of the Catholic Church in America. That assimilation and inculturation have taken place no serious student of American Catholicism doubts. In many ways, that has been a good and necessary thing. But in other respects, also to be discussed here, the results are deeply troubling.

As a sociological, psychological, and even spiritual process, Americanization was bound to happen. But it did not have to happen just as it did, nor must all the results now be accepted just as they stand. American Catholicism today is changing, and it will continue to change. As it does, two linked questions become more and more pressing: How American—in contemporary secular terms—can Catholics afford to become without compromising their Catholic identity; and must the future of Catholicism in the United States be more Americanization as we've experienced it up to now, or do we have other, better options?

Depending on who's answering them, replies to these questions differ enormously.

A cheerleader for Americanization, historian Jay P. Dolan, who taught at Notre Dame for many years, insists that "Catholicism and American culture can indeed complement and enrich each other.... [Catholicism] has found a home in the United States."[4] But compare that with this assessment by Francis Cardinal George of Chicago, president of the U.S. Conference of Catholic Bishops from 2007 to 2010: "While the Church in the United States enjoys a certain institutional freedom, she exists in a culture that, in often surprising ways, resists Catholicism."[5] A pastor I know states the practical consequences in blunt terms: "There's not a dime's worth of difference between Catholics and their fellow Americans now in moral outlook or religious practice. We fornicate at the same rate. We divorce at the same rate. We abort our children at the same rate. We are materially rich, and so, in true chauvinistic fashion, we claim favored-nation status before the Lord."

Jay Dolan, Cardinal George, and the pastor can't all be right.

My own view is that the current situation of American Catholicism is alarming, with the future a matter of deep concern. The Mass attendance rate in the United States on any given Sunday (or, more precisely, Saturday evening plus Sunday) is now 30% or less nationwide; in the 1950s and 1960s it was around 75%. Similar sharp declines in participation in the rest of the Church's sacramental life have also taken place—baptisms, confirmations, and Catholic marriages

---

[4] Jay P. Dolan, *In Search of an American Catholicism: A History of Religion and Culture in Tension* (New York: Oxford University Press, 2002), 11.

[5] Francis George, O.M.I., *The Difference God Makes: A Catholic Vision of Faith, Communion, and Culture* (New York: Crossroad, 2009), 28.

are all down. Three Catholics out of four receive the sacrament of penance ("go to confession") less than once a year—or never.

Vocations to the priesthood and religious life have plummeted, along with a corresponding drop in the number of clergy and persons in consecrated life and steep rises in the median age of members of each group. Poll results repeatedly show that the attitudes, values, and practices of many, possibly most, American Catholics—including attitudes toward the Church—mirror secular American attitudes, values, and behaviors rather than those of their Catholic tradition.[6] I shall return to the statistics and their implications in the final chapter of this book. Here it's enough to say that the picture the numbers paint is anything but good.

To be sure, American Catholicism's numbers are more robust than those for the Church in most of western Europe, where secularization has taken hold with a vengeance. But to say the Catholic Church in the United States is generally healthier than she is in countries like Spain, Switzerland, Germany, France, Belgium, the Netherlands, and now even Ireland is to say very little for it. And, comparisons aside, the numbers make it clear that American Catholicism isn't doing so well either.

Americanization isn't the only reason. Many factors have combined to produce this crisis. The scandal of sexual abuse of children and young people by some Catholic priests and

[6] A helpful, fairly recent overview of a number of studies and polls: William V. D'Antonio, James D. Davidson, Dean R. Hoge, and Mary L. Gautier, *American Catholics Today: New Realities of Their Faith and Their Church* (Lanham, Md.: Rowman and Littlefield, 2007). The latest updating of these data by D'Antonio and others was published in 2011. See "Catholics in America", *National Catholic Reporter*, October 28–November 10, 2011. Many helpful studies also are available on the website of the Center for Applied Research in the Apostolate at www.cara.georgetown.edu.

its cover-up by some bishops has done much to erode confidence in the Church (or anyway its leaders). Of fundamental importance too is the pervasive reality called secularization, which poses a serious challenge to Christianity just about everywhere today. But Americanization—the process of becoming part of the dominant secular culture of the United States—is a large part of what has happened. This book is concerned with Americanization's impact on American Catholicism, not apart from but together with factors like secularization and the sex abuse scandal.

Emphasizing Americanization explains why it makes sense to speak of the present situation of the Church in the United States as the Gibbons Legacy. Cardinal James Gibbons was far from being the only Americanizer in the history of American Catholicism, but Americanization wouldn't have achieved such widespread acceptance without his patronage and encouragement. John Ireland of Saint Paul was more flamboyant and pugnacious; John Keane of Richmond, Dubuque, and the Catholic University of America more intellectual; Denis O'Connell, rector of the American College in Rome, more immediately involved in day-in, day-out politicking. But by patient, quiet diplomacy that won him trust in Rome and respect even among his opponents, James Gibbons of Baltimore did more than anyone to further the Americanist project. Monsignor Ellis admiringly credits him with *discretio rationis*—the sense of reasonable proportion in judgment that Saint Thomas Aquinas held to be the most important virtue of those who govern: "It was that quality that raised the execution of policies by the cardinal to the level of statesmanship."[7] For better or worse—or, probably, both—American Catholicism even now is living on the Gibbons Legacy.

[7] Ellis, *Gibbons*, 2:647.

All the same, neither the Americanist project nor the controversy it provoked began with Cardinal Gibbons. Instead
we can start the story with Isaac Hecker and Orestes Brownson. Between them, they marked out the issues in this argument with remarkable clarity over a century and a half ago.

America in the middle years of the nineteenth century
was vastly different from America today, but many things
that exercised Brownson, Hecker, and their contemporaries
have present-day parallels: for crassness and consumerism then,
crassness and consumerism now; for anti-Catholic nativ-
ism, anti-Christian secular humanism; for ethnic conflict
between Catholic Irish-Americans and Catholic German-
Americans, ideological conflict between Catholic progressives and Catholic traditionalists; for slavery and the Civil
War, abortion and the culture war. And, for Catholics both
then and now, the pros and cons of an Americanist Church.

The Brownson-Hecker relationship has been called one
of the great stories of American Catholic history, but even
those who know the story often fail to grasp its underlying
significance. In their collaboration and also in their conflict, these two unusual men framed what remains the perennial question for Catholics in the United States: Can Catholics
be both fully American and also faithfully Catholic?

Orestes Brownson was born in Stockbridge, Vermont,
on September 16, 1803. His father died when he was two,
and the boy was separated from his mother and four sib-
lings and raised by an elderly couple who were nonpracticing Congregationalists.

Although Brownson received almost no formal school-
ing, he had a powerful intellect and was a voracious reader
and a resolute autodidact. Obsessed with religion from an
early age, he found the flux of new religious ideas and movements that dominated the kaleidoscope of American religion

in the 1820s and 1830s very much to his taste. First he tried Presbyterianism—then Universalism (he was a Universalist minister at several places in upstate New York), then Unitarianism, and even, for a short time in Boston, his own "Church of the Future".

In Boston he joined the transcendentalists. Major figures in America's religious avant-garde—Emerson, Bronson Alcott, Margaret Fuller, and others—were now Brownson's mentors, colleagues, and friends, and he rapidly acquired a reputation as an editor, writer, and popular lecturer. In 1837 he launched a journal called *Boston Quarterly Review*. By the 1840s he was a national figure with a substantial audience.

In late 1841 or early 1842 Brownson had a life-changing religious experience that left him profoundly aware of what he called the "freedom of God". God, he explained, is "not a resistless fate, an iron necessity, inaccessible to human prayer ... but a kind and merciful Father who hears when his children cry, and is ready, able, and willing to supply all their wants".[8] Resuming his religious quest, he discovered Catholicism, and on October 20, 1844, he was formally received into the Catholic Church. This was something his old friends found inexplicable on any grounds except his well-known changeability. In his *Fable for Critics* (1848), poet James Russell Lowell, after speaking of Emerson and Alcott, wrote of Brownson:

He shifts quite about, then proceeds to expound
That 'tis merely the earth, not himself, that turns round,
And wishes it clearly impressed on your mind
That the weathercock rules and not follows the wind.

---

[8] Quoted in Patrick W. Carey, *Orestes A. Brownson: American Religious Weathervane* (Grand Rapids, Mich.; Eerdmans, 2004), 101.

Isaac Hecker, 16 years younger and a disciple of Brownson since 1841, preceded the older man into the Catholic Church by several months. After Brownson's death in 1876, Hecker wrote Brownson's children: "I owe much, and more, to your father than to any other man in my early life."[9] Born December 18, 1819, in New York, he too was a religious seeker—as well as a mystic, whose life was changed in his early twenties by the vision of "a beautiful angelic pure being".[10] Like other young seekers who found their way to Brook Farm, he was influenced by the radical individualism of Emerson; but as he worked his way into Christianity and toward Catholicism, this enthusiasm cooled. Emerson, he concluded, had "no conception of the Church".[11] After his conversion, Hecker joined the Redemptorist order, and on October 23, 1849, he was ordained a Catholic priest.

From early in their Catholic years Brownson and Hecker shared the conviction that the United States was a promising setting for Catholic evangelization. Even so, temperamental differences tended to draw them apart. Hecker complained that Brownson "defeats but will never convince an opponent. . . . No one loves to break a lance with him because he leaves such ungentlemanly gashes."[12] Hecker, by contrast, was a man of great charm whom even people who disagreed with his ideas rarely disliked.

Commitment to the ideal of evangelizing America inevitably brought both men into conflict with others who held different views regarding midcentury Catholic priorities. For Brownson, the conflict centered on the pugnacious archbishop

[9] Quoted in David J. O'Brien, *Isaac Hecker: An American Catholic* (New York: Paulist Press, 1992), 256.
[10] Quoted in ibid., 19.
[11] Ibid., 56.
[12] Quoted in ibid., 79.

of New York, "Dagger John" Hughes. Brownson had moved there in 1845 and relaunched his journal under the name *Brownson's Quarterly Review*. Hughes, who regarded mass conversions of Protestants as an unrealistic goal with no practical bearing on the urgent needs of his immigrant flock, reportedly told him, "I want no one in my diocese I can't control." Taking the hint, Brownson moved himself and his journal to the friendlier precincts of Elizabeth, New Jersey.

For his part, Hecker was stymied by what he considered the ethnic narrowness and cramped vision of his Redemptorist brothers, whom he found to be more intent on giving missions and doing parish work among German immigrants than converting members of the New England intellectual elite whom Hecker had known at Brook Farm. In August 1857, uninvited, he journeyed to Rome to plead his case with the order's leaders; there, depending on how one chooses to interpret the series of events that followed, he either quit the Redemptorists or was expelled. But his pleasing personality and evident sincerity had won him highly placed friends, including Pope Pius IX. Returning to the United States, in 1858 he founded the Missionary Society of Saint Paul—the Paulists—with a nucleus of ex-Redemptorists as its first members.

Although Orestes Brownson is sometimes described as a political and religious liberal, his views, true to his weathercock nature, continued to shift even after he entered the Catholic Church. Eventually he became a crotchety old man, but at least as early as 1857, long before the crotchets of age set in, he was taking issue with central elements of Hecker's proto-Americanism.

Hecker's first book, *Questions of the Soul*, published in 1855, had established him as a prominent Catholic spokesman and earned him a national reputation. Appearing two years later, his second, *Aspirations of Nature*, declared the United States to be an "unfettered civilization" ready for conversion ("true Religion will find a reception it has in vain looked for elsewhere").[13] To the disappointment of the idealistic author, *Aspirations* received much less attention and approval than *Questions*. Particularly galling was Brownson's skeptical review.

The number of "earnest seekers" in the United States, Brownson wrote, was far less than Hecker supposed, and those most likely to be attracted to Catholicism were evangelical Protestants, not members of the post-Christian Brook Farm set who interested Hecker. In any case, the conversion of America would be far from easy, since there was "scarcely a trait in the American character as practically developed that is not more or less hostile to Catholicity". Americans, Brownson held, were "imbued with a spirit of independence, an aversion to authority, a pride, an overwhelming conceit, as well as with a prejudice that makes them revolt at the bare mention of the Church".[14]

Hecker was surprised and hurt. Although their friendship survived the shock, and although Brownson wrote for Hecker's new magazine, the *Catholic World*, their relationship was never again the same. But the great parting of the ways did not come until early in the 1870s.

By then, both men had long outgrown the naïve enthusiasm of new converts and had suffered hard knocks from life, including life in the Catholic Church. Deeply saddened by the loss of two sons in the Civil War, Brownson was disgusted by Catholic support for the South in that conflict. Gout and failing health plagued him. Having given up his

[13] Quoted in ibid., 117.
[14] Quoted in ibid., 122.

Quarterly Review, he chafed under editing at the *Catholic World* by men whom he regarded as dangerously liberal. A convinced ultramontanist by now, he declared himself "a convert to" Pius IX's Syllabus of Errors (1864), with its critique of much secular conventional wisdom of the day. "The bolder and more uncompromising the Church, the sounder is the policy", Brownson declared.[15] Intense dislike of anything resembling Catholic accommodationism fed his growing suspicion of Hecker and the Paulists.

Meanwhile, Hecker had problems of his own. Having wangled a place on the fringes of the First Vatican Council (1869–1870), he sided emotionally with the party of "inopportunists" who opposed defining the dogma of papal infallibility at that time. Strange to say, though, once infallibility had been defined, he warmly embraced it and declared that it would be helpful in evangelizing America. But few of his fellow Paulists seemed to have much interest in that great enterprise.

Matters came to a head over a letter Hecker wrote Brownson from Rome. Dated January 30, 1870, it cited the "increased interest and appreciation" for the United States that the writer reported finding among "men of all parties and schools in Europe". In view of this receptiveness, Hecker declared, "no greater service can be rendered" to the Europeans than to give them an account of "the relations of the Church to our free institutions".

> For the extension of political suffrage and places of power to the people is in no way hostile to the dogmas of the Catholic Religion. On the contrary, the more the responsibility is shared by the individuals who compose a nation,

---

[15] Quoted in Carey, *Brownson*, 294.

in its direction, the greater their merit and the greater the glory of God. . . .

This concession, will necessarily call forth from the Church a fresh zeal to instruct people to fulfill properly their new responsibilities. Thus giving an extension to her influence, adding a new title of gratitude for her services, and showing in a new light the absolute necessity of Religion for civil society & good government.[16]

Brownson wasn't impressed. For a long time he had suspected Hecker and his colleague at the *Catholic World*, Father Augustine Hewit, of holding views about the effects of original sin that bordered on heterodoxy. He was convinced that these effects went very deep, and this belief provided theological grounds for an increasingly skeptical view of American democracy, while Hecker's effusions struck him as jejune at best. Hardly less deplorable was Hecker's tendency to paper over differences with Protestants for the sake of finding common ground. From that perspective, he regarded his old friend's thinking as not merely fatuous but dangerous.

On August 25, 1870, Brownson wrote to Hecker in reply. Although he too had once sung the praises of American constitutional democracy ("The United States, or the American Republic, has a mission, and is chosen by God for the realization of a great idea" [17]), the tune was different now. While supporting the American system "because it is the legal & only practicable form", he said, "I no longer hope

---

[16] *The Brownson-Hecker Correspondence*, eds. Joseph F. Gower and Richard M. Leliaert (Notre Dame, Ind.: University of Notre Dame Press, 1979), 288.

[17] "Brownson Defines the World Mission of the American Republic, 1865" (excerpt from *The American Republic: Its Constitution, Tendencies, and Destiny*), in John Tracy Ellis, ed., *Documents of American Catholic History* (Milwaukee: Bruce, 1962), 384.

anything of it." This was especially so where the interests
of the Catholic Church were concerned.

> Instead of regarding the Church as having advantages here
> which she has nowhere else, I think she has here a more
> subtle and powerful enemy to combat than in any of the
> old monarchical nations of the world. Say what we will, we
> have made little impression on our old American popula-
> tion, & what little we have made we owe to the conviction
> that [the] Church sustains authority, demands government,
> is anti-radical, anti-democratic. . . .
>
> Catholics as well as others imbibe the spirit of the coun-
> try, imbibe from infancy the spirit of independence, free-
> dom from all restraint, unbounded license. So far are we
> from converting the country, we cannot hold our own. . . .
> How many Catholics can you find born & brought up in
> the country that do in reality hold the Church to be higher
> than the people, or who do not consider her voice author-
> itative only when it coincides with that of the people?
>
> These considerations make me feel that the whole influ-
> ence of democratic ideas & tendencies is directly antagonis-
> tic to Catholicity. I think the Church has never encountered
> a social & political order so hostile to her, & that the con-
> version of our republic will be a far greater victory than the
> conversion of the Roman Empire. . . . I have hitherto wished
> to effect a harmony of the American & the Catholic idea,
> but I believe such harmony impracticable except by sacri-
> ficing the Catholic idea to the National.[18]

Seldom before or since have the battle lines in the great debate
over Americanism and Americanization been drawn more
sharply than they'd now been drawn by Hecker and Brownson.

The professional relationship between the two men survived a while longer, but in January 1872 Brownson formally

---

[18] *Brownson-Hecker Correspondence*, 291–92.

resigned as a writer for the *Catholic World*. Habits of mutual affection nevertheless kept them on personally friendly terms until Brownson's death. By then he was living in Detroit with his son, Henry. After enjoying a table-thumping argument over the identity of the unpardonable sin, the old man took to his bed on Good Friday of 1876 and, having received the last rites of the Church, died on Easter Monday, April 17. By a twist of irony, Brownson today is buried in the crypt of the campus church of the University of Notre Dame, the flagship institution of the Americanist impulse in Catholic higher education.

Hecker lived on another twelve years, increasingly isolated within his own religious community, where few Paulists seemed to share his vision. His efforts as writer and lecturer had brought few converts into the Church. Despite his persistently optimistic vision of the future, he suffered intensely from depression—an "almost unceasing desolation of spirit"—that earlier had caused him to pass several curiously lethargic years in Europe.[19] On December 21, 1888, worn down by emotional illness and disappointed hopes—for the conversion of his country and for the religious institute he'd founded with that great project in view—he blessed the Paulists with whom he was living and passed away. On January 25, 2008, in a ceremony at the mother church of the Paulists, Saint Paul the Apostle on Fifty-Ninth Street, Edward Cardinal Egan of New York began an investigative process that could someday lead the Church, in her wisdom, to declare Isaac Hecker a saint. At this time he has the title Servant of God.

It would be foolish to declare either Hecker or Brownson the winner in their argument about America and the prospects of the Catholic Church. Each was badly wrong

---

[19] On Hecker's health, see O'Brien, *Isaac Hecker*, 259–60.

in part: Brownson's gloomy intransigence was an off-putting, tactical, and substantive mistake, while Hecker's too-easy optimism about human affairs—optimism that the sorrows of his later years diluted but didn't destroy—comes across now as childish and irritating. But each also was right about certain things, and it is conceivable that a new synthesis could be forged from these elements to guide the future course of the Church in America in notably troubled times. The outlines of such a program will emerge as we continue to examine the Gibbons Legacy.

Along with ideology, two powerful, interconnected forces helped speed the Americanization of American Catholicism in the nineteenth century: immigration and anti-Catholicism. Numbers hint in dry, abstract terms at the tremendous human and institutional impact that immigration had in these years on the Catholic community and the nation as a whole.

Earlier, Catholics had played notable roles in the American struggle for independence. These included native-born Americans like Charles Carroll of Carrollton and his brother, John, who was to become the first Catholic bishop in the United States, as well as foreigners like Lafayette and Kosciuśzko. As many as 50% of George Washington's troops had Irish surnames. At war's end, however, out of a total population of 4 million, there were only about 25,000 Catholics in the new nation, mostly in Maryland and Pennsylvania. The Catholics were served by a few dozen priests, almost all of them foreign born.

By 1820, the end of the republican era, the number of Catholics had crept up to 120,000. And then the immigration explosion began.

Between 1820 and 1870, 2.7 million Catholics came pouring into the country. Most were from Ireland, Germany, and France. The 1880s brought another 1.25 million, with Catholics from eastern and southern Europe—Poles, Ukrainians, Italians, and others—joining the influx. The newcomers fanned out rapidly, from the East Coast to other parts of the expanding nation, with new communities like Chicago, Milwaukee, and Saint Louis becoming important centers of Catholic population.

The first diocese in the United States, Baltimore, was established in 1789, with John Carroll as its bishop. At the time it covered the entire country. By 1840, the 663,000 Catholics in America lived in 15 dioceses and were served by 500 priests. By 1900, Catholics numbered 12 million in a population of 76 million; they were, and for some time had been, America's largest single religious denomination. They lived in 82 dioceses and were served by 12,000 priests along with many thousands of religious women and men.

The challenges of coping with this explosive growth are easy to imagine; in fact, it's remarkable in the circumstances that the leaders and people of the Church in America coped as well as they did. The seven provincial and three plenary councils of Baltimore held by the American bishops between 1829 and 1884 had a key role in this process. It was here, writes Joseph Varacalli, that the hierarchy developed the outlines of an American Catholic "plausibility structure" within which "doctrine was standardized, renegade clergy were disciplined, and churches, schools, hospitals and other infrastructural requirements were built." [20]

Nevertheless, the leadership of the Church in America had nothing to say collectively about the central moral issue

---

[20] Joseph A. Varacalli, *Bright Promise, Failed Community: Catholics and the American Public Order* (Lanham, Md.: Lexington Books, 2000), 56.

of the century, slavery, although Catholics disputed the question among themselves. The infamous *Dred Scott* decision of 1857, premised on the idea that slaves were not fully persons, was written by a Catholic, Chief Justice Roger Brooke Taney. And Catholics fought without apparent moral qualms on both sides of the Civil War.

The intracommunity conflicts among Catholics also were very real, with that between the Irish and the Germans perhaps the most serious as well as the one with the most obvious direct bearing on our subject here. At its heart it was a quarrel about assimilation and Americanization. As English speakers, the Irish enjoyed an obvious advantage in the race for ascendancy within the Church along with social acceptance and political influence, while the Germans lagged behind. Irish names quickly became conspicuous in the ranks of the hierarchy, while Irishmen pressed the drive for Catholic entry into the American mainstream. As a result, the Church in America was sometimes described as one, holy, Irish, and apostolic. In Saint Louis, a place where German priests outnumbered Irish, 11 out of 12 priests promoted to bishop between 1854 and 1924 were of Irish extraction.

Looking back, it's clear that the Germans had some legitimate grievances, but at the time churchmen like James Gibbons—born in 1834 as the first son of an Irish immigrant family in Baltimore—were apparently not moved by their claims. A Saint Patrick's Day sermon preached by Gibbons in 1871 is a striking illustration of Hibernian triumphalism in which the speaker not only acknowledges but celebrates Irish hegemony in the American hierarchy while declaring the victimization of the Irish in their homeland and their exodus to the New World to have been part of God's providential plan to have them contribute so much "to the establishment and prosperity of the greatest Republic in the world".[21]

German Catholics predictably complained to Rome that their pastoral needs were being neglected and battled to retain the language, rituals, and customs of the old country—their German cultural identity, that is. Gibbons, Ireland, and their fellow Americanizers fought back and argued the case for assimilation. In time, assimilation won out, as it was bound to do, and the Germans also were Americanized. "But the nationality debate never really ended", Jay Dolan observes. "The French from Quebec likewise fought to preserve *la langue et la foi*; the Polish, Italians, Slovaks, and numerous other groups waged similar battles."[22] In the early decades of the twenty-first century, it's an open question how this old story will play out now among the fast-growing population of Latino Catholics in the United States, said to be approaching 30 million in number as this is written and in the foreseeable future likely to be a majority of American Catholics.

Immigration fueled conflict not just within the Church but also between Catholics and other elements in American society. Periodic upsurges of anti-Catholicism were the result. *The Awful Disclosures of Maria Monk*, a volume full of lurid tales of convent life, was published in 1835, becoming a best seller second only to the Bible in American publishing history. Purporting to be the work of an ex-nun, the book was written by Protestant ministers. The year before it appeared, an Ursuline convent in Charlestown, Massachusetts, was attacked and burned by a mob seeking to free

[21] "The Apostolic Mission of the Irish Race", sermon preached March 17, 1871, in *A Retrospect of Fifty Years* (Baltimore: John Murphy, 1916), 2:177.
[22] Dolan, *In Search*, 98.

a woman supposedly being held there against her will. In Philadelphia, thirteen people died and two churches and a school were burned during nativist riots in 1844. In New York, however, Archbishop "Dagger John" Hughes ringed the city's Catholic churches with armed Irishmen and promised that New York would go up in flames if there was trouble.

The 1850s brought the Know-Nothing movement, so called because its adherents were instructed to reply to inquiries by saying they knew nothing about the group, whose aim was to exclude from public office foreigners and Catholics—in many places, very nearly one and the same thing. The Know-Nothings remained a significant political force in America until about 1860. If those people ever came to power, Lincoln remarked to a friend, the Declaration of Independence would have to be rewritten to read, "All men are created equal except negroes, foreigners, and Catholics." [23]

Anti-Catholicism wasn't limited to angry mobs and Know-Nothings; sophisticated sectors of American society sometimes exploited the same themes. I am the proud owner of a notable anti-Catholic artifact of those times—a Thomas Nast cartoon. The German-born Nast was a cartoonist of genius who created a number of lasting images—the classic depiction of Santa Claus as a fat, jolly man (he'd been tall and skinny until then); the Republican elephant and the Democratic donkey; and Columbia, pictured as a gowned woman wearing a tiara and carrying a sword. Between 1862 and 1886 his work appeared regularly in *Harper's Weekly*.

Along with being a brilliant cartoonist, Nast was a bitter anti-Catholic. My sample of his work is a framed page from

[23] Quoted in John Tracy Ellis, *American Catholicism*, rev. 2nd ed. (Chicago: University of Chicago Press, 1969), 86.

the February 19, 1870, *Harper's Weekly* bearing the title "Church and State".[24] The drawing is a skillfully nasty piece of work combining racism with religious bigotry. It was inspired by the angry controversy of those years focused on Catholic efforts to obtain public funds for parochial schools. But the cartoonist's distaste for Catholics cuts a broad swath extending far beyond that one issue.

In the cartoon's top panel, Pope Pius IX sags disconsolately in the arms of mitered clerics as Lady Liberty tears apart a scroll whose two halves bear the words "Church" and "State". Looking on with approval are European political leaders of the day, among them Queen Victoria and Chancellor Bismarck. In the lower panel, set in the United States, a beaming Pius IX blesses an ugly crone who is busily stitching "Church" and "State" back together. Liberty, in manacles, glowers from a pillar emblazoned "Fraudulent Votes" while a lout with brutish cartoon-Irish features mocks her plight. At one side of the drawing, a chubby priest happily accepts a sack labeled "Public School Money". A similar scene is being enacted in the background, where a cowled monk flourishes a crucifix and a top-hatted Irishman brandishes an axe.

With propaganda like this common fare in a leading secular journal of the day, Catholics felt impelled to react. One form that took was strenuous affirmation of the compatibility of Catholicism and the American tradition. The naming of the Knights of Columbus is a poignant illustration of that.

---

[24] The *Harper's Weekly* page was given to me by a friend to celebrate a novel, also called *Church and State*, that I published in 1979. The book tells of events during a presidential campaign some years in the future that bear a surprising resemblance to events in 1976, when leaders of the American bishops' conference took an active role in the presidential campaign of that year in support of a pro-life amendment to the U.S. Constitution. (See below, pp. 149–51.) If Nast had been living then, those few weeks would have supplied material for his talented, vitriolic pen.

The Knights of Columbus was founded in New Haven in early 1882 by a young Irish-American priest, Father Michael J. McGivney, and a group of Catholic laymen. The basement of Saint Mary's Church, located a short walk from the New Haven green, was its humble birthplace. Just a few years before, the dedication of this Catholic church in a well-to-do residential section of the city was the occasion for a "there goes the neighborhood" account published in the *New York Times*.

The founders of the Knights of Columbus had modest ambitions: a local fraternal insurance society offering members an attractive death benefit feature to provide for widows and orphans. Beyond that, they also hoped to give Catholic men an alternative to joining the Masons and other groups in which they were at risk of being weaned away from their faith.

But what to call the new Catholic organization? Various names were considered and rejected. In the end, Knights of Columbus won out. It was an inspired choice—"profoundly significant", Christopher J. Kauffman calls it in his history of the Knights. "By adopting Columbus as their patron, this small group of New Haven Irish-American Catholics displayed their pride in America's Catholic heritage. The name Columbus evoked the aura of Catholicity and affirmed the discovery of America as a Catholic event.... 'Knights' symbolizes the deep conviction that to pledge one's fealty to the Catholic ideals of Columbus involved one in a militant struggle against the strong anti-Catholic and, therefore, anti-Irish sentiment so prevalent in traditional New England society." [25]

[25] Christopher J. Kauffman, *Faith and Fraternalism: The History of the Knights of Columbus, 1882–1982* (New York: Harper and Row, 1982), 16–17.

Blunting anti-Catholicism was one prong of the Americanist impulse among nineteenth-century Catholics. The other, positive in intentions and content, was to sing the praises of the United States as a providentially provided home for the Church. The most prominent, wholehearted, and full-throated proponent of this point of view, surpassing even Isaac Hecker, was John Ireland, archbishop of Saint Paul from 1884 until his death in 1918.

Addressing his colleagues in the hierarchy at the Third Plenary Council of Baltimore in 1884, Ireland underlined the mutual advantages that he saw flowing from friendly relations between the nation and the Catholic Church:

> [T]he choicest field which providence offers in the world today to the occupancy of the Church is this republic, and she welcomes with delight the signs of the times that indicate a glorious future for her beneath the starry banner. But it is true, also, the surest safeguards for her own life and prosperity the republic will find in the teachings of the Catholic Church, and the more America acknowledges those teachings, the more durable will her civil institutions be made.

Here was no mere marriage of convenience; rather, as Ireland saw it, the United States and the Catholic Church were meant for each other. And for this, he told a French audience in 1892, the Church had great reason to be thankful to God.

> If in America the Catholic Church does not make progress, it is not the fault of the republic.... The republic allows the Church the fullest liberty; and the Church, conscious of her divine mission, feels within herself all the vital forces necessary to grow and conquer without alliance with, or aid from, the state.... [T]hose who differ with us in faith, have no distrust of Catholic bishops and priests. Why should they? By word and act we prove that we are patriots of

patriots. Our hearts always beat with love for the republic.
Our tongues are always eloquent in celebrating her praises.
Our hands are always uplifted to bless her banners and her
soldiers.[26]

Ireland, who had served as a chaplain with the Union army
during the Civil War, was himself conspicuous in demon-
strating his point by word and act.

As embodied in powerful churchmen like Ireland and Gibbons, Americanism had several principal articles of faith:
that the world was undergoing radical change (as indeed
was true then and remains true today); that America was at
the cutting edge of change (as undoubtedly was true in the
days of Gibbons and Ireland and remains true—though perhaps less clearly so—even now); that there was a fundamental and intrinsic compatibility between Catholicism and
American culture; and that the Church in America had a
God-given duty to show the rest of the Church, and especially her leadership in Rome, the way to the future as that
path was then being marked out in the United States (which
contained, and may still contain, important elements of truth
but which suffers from the fatal arrogance of American
exceptionalism dressed in ecclesiastical garb).

John Ireland believed these things with all his heart. Orestes
Brownson had once believed them but no longer did at the
end. And Catholics today? The jury is divided about that.

It's impossible to read an account of American Catholicism around the turn of the twentieth century or the biography of any prominent Catholic ecclesiastical figure of

[26] John Ireland, "Archbishop John Ireland: America in France", in Coleman J. Barry, O.S.B., ed., *Readings in Church History* (Westminster, Md.: Christian Classics, 1985), 1067–68.

that era without encountering the name Denis O'Connell—usually many times. Monsignor O'Connell turns up repeatedly, a familiar presence in Rome, providing news and insider speculation, passing along gossip, sharing sharp-tongued judgments about mutual enemies, and egging on the leaders of the liberal, Americanist wing of the hierarchy back home in the United States. As tensions between the Holy See and the Americanists mount, O'Connell more and more can be seen becoming a ubiquitous behind-the-scenes presence representing the interests of Americanism. Contemporaries called him "Machiavelli", sometimes affectionately and sometimes not.[27] It's easy to see why. A protégé and close friend of Cardinal Gibbons, O'Connell was rector of the American College in Rome during the crucial decade 1885 to 1895. He also was the American bishops' agent at the Holy See, a role that as time passed O'Connell increasingly interpreted to mean being an agent of the Americanists—Gibbons, Ireland, Keane, et al.—against conservative opponents like Archbishop Corrigan of New York and Bishop McQuaid of Rochester.

In a letter of December 10, 1898, written from Paris to Father Walter Elliott, Paulist priest and biographer of Isaac Hecker, O'Connell happily shared an upbeat piece of insider information: "Now it appears, and appears certain, that there will be no encyclical at all."[28] This was great good news for the Americanists, since "no encyclical" meant no papal condemnation of Americanism.

[27] See Gerald P. Fogarty, S.J., *The Vatican and the Americanist Crisis: Denis J. O'Connell, American Agent in Rome, 1885–1903* (Rome: Università Gregoriana Editrice, 1974), 90.

[28] Quoted in Gerald P. Fogarty, S.J., *The Vatican and the Americanist Crisis: Denis J. O'Connell, American Agent in Rome, 1885–1903* (Rome: Università Gregoriana Editrice, 1974), 286.

O'Connell was frequently well informed, but he wasn't always right. On January 22, 1899, Pope Leo XIII dispatched to Gibbons a document cast in the form of a letter; it bore the title *Testem benevolentiae* (In witness to goodwill). "Therefore, from what We have said thus far," the pope wrote, "it is clear, Our Beloved Son, that those opinions cannot be approved by us the sum total of which some indicate by the name of Americanism."[29]

Appalled, Gibbons held up the document's release in the United States for a week, until the publication of excerpts originating overseas forced his hand and moved him to give it to the *Baltimore Sun*. "We have done our utmost" to prevent publication of the papal letter, Bishop Keane remarked glumly.[30] The bishops of the Milwaukee province, a center of German-American Catholicism, said that the errors condemned by Pope Leo really did exist. To Denis O'Connell, Cardinal Gibbons wrote: "[I]t is very discouraging to us that the American Church is not understood abroad, & that its enemies are listened to, & that they can lie with impunity."[31]

The tangled story of Americanism's condemnation has often been told and needn't be repeated in detail here. In general, it's as follows.

As angry rhetoric and troubling reports drifted to Rome from the United States during the 1890s, apprehension grew at the Vatican concerning conditions in the Church in America as well as concerning the influence American-style Catholicism was having on Catholicism in Europe

---

[29] Pope Leo XIII, *Testem benevolentiae*, January 22, 1899, in Henry Denziger, *The Sources of Catholic Dogma*, trans. Roy J. Deferrari (St. Louis: B. Herder, 1957), 500.

[30] Quoted in Ellis, *Gibbons*, 2:66.

[31] Quoted in ibid., 70.

and especially in France. America, with its democratic system of governance and its doctrine of church-state separation, had for a long time been worrisome in Roman eyes. As the nineteenth century drew to a close, this old anxiety hardened into suspicion of the Americanists and their French admirers.

In January 1895 Pope Leo fired a warning shot across the Americanist bow in the form of a letter to the Church in the United States called *Longinqua oceani*. Brimming with praise for America and American Catholicism, it nevertheless cautioned against things like divorce and secret societies and pointedly called it wrong to suppose that separation of church and state was "the most desirable status of the Church" or would be "universally lawful or expedient" everywhere.[32] The message to the Americanists was: Don't push too hard!

Infighting intensified in the next several years, along with Pope Leo's concern. The immediate occasion for the publication of *Testem benevolentiae* appears to have been the publication of a French translation of a condensation of the *Life of Isaac Thomas Hecker* by Walter Elliott, the American Paulist mentioned above. The volume also contained a lengthy, provocative preface by Felix Klein, a liberal French priest and lecturer at the Institut catholique. Published in 1896, the book went through six printings in a matter of months and touched off a heated controversy.

Hailing Hecker as an exemplary priest for the times, Klein situated the American among the "great religious figures" of history, while setting out his ideas with what one Hecker biographer calls "considerable exaggeration".[33] Among them

---

[32] Quoted in ibid., 28.
[33] O'Brien, *Hecker*, 383.

was the view that people should place direct personal reliance upon the indwelling of the Holy Spirit and that spiritual directors should encourage them to this end, an "American idea ... [that Hecker] knew to be God's will for all civilized people of our time".

It is an interesting question whether the opinions singled out for criticism in *Testem benevolentiae* were Hecker's, Elliott's, or Klein's, or those of all three, but that needn't detain us here. Pope Leo collectively called them Americanism, and he condemned them. Klein much later declared Americanism to be a "phantom heresy",[34] but the French edition of the Hecker biography was quickly withdrawn, and that, for the most part, was the end of "theological" Americanism in Europe. As we shall see, the story was different in the United States.

Historians friendly to Americanism typically take their lead from Klein and dismiss both the "phantom heresy" and Leo XIII's condemnation of it. The contents of *Testem benevolentiae* receive less than a page and a half in the 80-page chapter titled "Americanism" in John Tracy Ellis' massive biography of Cardinal Gibbons, and the summary Ellis gives there might charitably be described as superficial. But the pope's critique is more substantial than apologists for the Americanists like Monsignor Ellis choose to recognize. In fact, much that *Testem benevolentiae* says is pertinent to current conditions in U.S. Catholicism.

One set of ideas condemned by Leo XIII concerns placing natural virtues above supernatural ones, along with a division of virtues into "passive" and "active" that assigns preference to the latter as supposedly more suited to modern

---

[34] In 1949, Klein, then 87, published the fourth volume of his *Souvenirs*, with the title *Une Hérésie Fantôme, L'Americanisme.*

times. This is said to lead to a certain "contempt ... for the religious life" [35] and to the disparagement of religious vows. If that were all there was to Americanism as it's described in *Testem benevolentiae*, it might be taken as a Victorian precursor of the crisis afflicting religious life in the United States during the years since Vatican Council II—a serious matter, that is, yet comparatively limited in scope.

That, however, was by no means all that troubled Pope Leo. His concerns focused especially on the "basis of the new opinions" converging in Americanism. Saying it arose from a desire to attract to the Catholic Church "those who dissent", Leo summed it up in these words: "[T]he Church should come closer to the civilization of this advanced age, and relaxing its old severity show indulgence to those opinions and theories of the people which have recently been introduced." Lest anyone be uncertain about what that meant, the pope added that "many" believed the relaxation should extend even to "the doctrines in which the deposit of faith is contained". But already, he insisted, the Magisterium of the Church was as flexible as fidelity to divine revelation would allow. Furthermore, the norm of flexibility was "not to be determined by the decision of private individuals.... [I]t should be the judgment of the Church." Opposed to this orthodox understanding, and prominent among the errors of the day, was the view that "the faithful may indulge ... each one his own mind" inasmuch as nowadays the Holy Spirit was bestowing "more and richer gifts than in times past"—a largesse empowering everyone to settle matters of belief for himself by "a kind of hidden instinct".[36]

---

[35] *Testem benevolentiae*, in Denziger, *Sources of Catholic Dogma*, 500–511.
[36] Ibid., 499–500.

This is heavy criticism. And Leo XIII's closing words are heavier still.

> Therefore, from what we have said thus far it is clear, Our Beloved Son, that those opinions cannot be approved by us, the sum total of which some indicate by the name of Americanism. . . . For it raises a suspicion that there are those among you who envision and desire a Church in America other than that which is in all the rest of the world.
>
> One in unity of doctrine as in unity of government and this Catholic, such is the Church; and since God has established that its center and foundation be in the Chair of Peter, it is rightly called Roman.[37]

Seeking consolation where he could find it, Cardinal Gibbons assured Monsignor O'Connell that the pope's letter had "excited scarcely any comment in the secular papers, & the Cath. papers as far as received have little to say about it except that they don't see its application to our country."[38] Still, Gibbons and his friends truly were rattled. Since *Testem benevolentiae* was addressed to him, a reply from the cardinal was in order. On March 17, 1899, he sent Leo XIII the following response.

> The letter in which Your Holiness reproves the errors which certain persons have represented under the name of Americanism reached me towards the middle of February. I had an English translation made which I published along with the Latin text.
>
> My feelings are too well known to Your Holiness for me to have to say that I thank you with my whole heart for having cast light on all these questions, which, in circles outside the United States, certain people seemed to enjoy

[37] Ibid., 500.
[38] Quoted in Ellis, *Gibbons*, 2:70.

complicating during the past year, but which in this country count for nothing in public opinion.

This doctrine, which I deliberately call extravagant and absurd, this Americanism as it has been called, has nothing in common with the views, aspirations, doctrine and conduct of Americans. I do not think that there can be found in the entire country a bishop, a priest, or even a layman with a knowledge of his religion who has ever uttered such enormities. No, that is not—it never has been and never will be—our Americanism. I am deeply grateful to Your Holiness for having yourself made this distinction in your apostolic letter.

I wanted to write at once to Your Holiness to thank you for this new act of kindness in our regard, but I preferred to wait in order to judge the effect which the papal document would have on public opinion and in particular on American Catholics. I am happy, Most Holy Father, to be able to tell you that the attitude which has been expressed, while mixed with certain surprise that such doctrines could have been attributed to American Catholics, has been one of the most profound respect for the mind of the Holy See, of lively gratitude for the kindness which you show us, of sincere appreciation for the distinction which Your Holiness so justly makes between the doctrines which we, along with you, reject, and those feelings of love for our country and its institutions which we share with our fellow citizens and which are such a powerful aid in accomplishing our work for the glory of God and the honor of Holy Church.[39]

Pope Leo XIII died on July 20, 1903, after one of the longest pontificates in history—25 years in the Chair of Peter. A year before his death, in "personal reminiscences" delivered in the Baltimore cathedral, Cardinal Gibbons paid the

[39] Text in ibid., 71.

old pope copious tribute, with particular attention given to three of his encyclicals, which he called "masterly and luminous".[40] The three included the 1891 social encyclical *Rerum novarum*, which Gibbons' intervention with Rome so many years before on behalf of the Knights of Labor had helped to shape, and two others—but not a word about *Testem benevolentiae* and the condemnation of Americanism.

Indeed, it seems unlikely that the religiously tinged chauvinism of men like Gibbons and Ireland had much immediate connection with the theological views condemned by Leo XIII. These were practical men, builders and doers, not theorists, and they wished to be loyal to the Church and to the pope. But there's more to the story than that. Better than Pope Leo or anyone else could have known at the time, the principal opinions condemned in *Testem benevolentiae* have by now become central elements in the ongoing debate about Catholic identity and the future of the Church in the United States. In this, Leo XIII's letter was far ahead of its times.

So, for instance, *Testem benevolentiae* skewers the idea that "the faithful may indulge ... each one his own mind" in matters of doctrine and morality inasmuch as the Holy Spirit showers present-day Catholics with "more and richer gifts than in times past", thus giving individuals "a kind of hidden instinct" for deciding the truth in religious matters. Reading that, one thinks of all the post–Vatican II loose talk about things like *sensus fidelium* and discernment. Much has been said about the gifts of the Spirit in the years since Vatican II, and of course the Spirit does give many gifts to

[40] James Cardinal Gibbons, "Personal Reminiscences of Pope Leo XIII: Sermon Preached in Baltimore Cathedral, April 2, 1902", in *A Retrospect of Fifty Years* (Baltimore: John Murphy, 1916), 2:83.

the Church. But it is questionable whether he commonly gives them to isolated individuals with a chip on their shoulder in regard to the Magisterium. By now, in fact, it's become perfectly clear that the casual invoking of the Spirit is in many cases no more than a rhetorical device opening the door to what often is called cafeteria Catholicism—that pick-and-choose selectivity in matters of belief and practice now common among American Catholics. We shall see more about this below.

As a coda to this overview, the relationship between Americanism and Modernism deserves a few words. First of all, though, was there a relationship? Monsignor Ellis says Modernism's impact on the Church in the United States was "on the whole slight and of relatively secondary importance".[41] Very likely that was true of the early years of the twentieth century, the time frame of which Ellis is speaking, but since Ellis wrote there has been a resurgence of Modernist or neo-Modernist thought that he did not anticipate. Yet, as studies by scholars like R. Scott Appleby and Christopher Kauffman have shown, even within Monsignor Ellis' arbitrarily defined context, Americanism and Modernism had more than casual links.[42] The extent and the limitations of these deserve our attention.

First, though, some readers' memories may today need refreshing on the subject of Modernism. Briefly put, this is the name given to a collection of ideas that in the late

---

[41] Ellis, *Gibbons*, 2:170.

[42] See R. Scott Appleby, *"Church and Age Unite!": The Modernist Impulse in American Catholicism* (Notre Dame, Ind.: University of Notre Dame Press, 1992), and Christopher J. Kauffman, *Tradition and Transformation in Catholic Culture: The Priests of Saint Sulpice in the United States from 1791 to the Present* (New York: Macmillan, 1988).

nineteenth and early twentieth centuries were identified with a loosely tied group of Catholic intellectuals located mostly in France, Italy, and England. Its best-known figures were the French Scripture scholar Alfred Loisy and the Irish Jesuit George Tyrrell; Tyrrell was excommunicated in 1907, Loisy in 1908. Others associated with Modernism included the historian Louis Duchesne, the novelist Antonio Fogazzaro, the philosopher Maurice Blondel (who was genuinely horrified at being thought at odds with the Church), and the pietistic German British intellectual gadfly Baron Friedrich von Hugel. Modernism received its name from the man who condemned it, Pope Saint Pius X.

Modernist themes were drawn from various turn-of-the-century sources of religious speculation. Marvin R. O'Connell, in his balanced history of the movement, calls an anonymous document called *Il programma di modernisti*—probably the work of an Italian philosopher and editor named Ernesto Buonaiuti—"perhaps the most succinct and coherent statement of the Modernist position ever attempted".[43] Among the principal elements of Modernism identified there are immanentism—the idea that religion expresses a human need rather than conveys divine revelation ("Religion is ... the spontaneous result of irrepressible needs of man's spirit, which find satisfaction in the inward and emotional experience of the presence of God within us")—and evolution, said to provide the only basis for believing in "the permanence of something divine in the life of the Church".[44]

[43] Marvin R. O'Connell, *Critics on Trial: An Introduction to the Catholic Modernist Crisis* (Washington, D.C.: Catholic University of America Press, 1994), 358–59.

[44] Quoted in ibid., 358, 359. One is reminded of Blessed John Henry Newman's words about religious liberalism, on the occasion of his formal designation as a cardinal in 1879: "Liberalism in religion is the doctrine that there

On July 3, 1907, the Vatican's Holy Office, forerunner of today's Congregation for the Doctrine of the Faith, issued a decree named *Lamentabili* listing and condemning 65 propositions found contrary to Catholic orthodoxy. Two months later, on September 8, Pope Pius followed with an encyclical, *Pascendi Dominici gregis* (Feeding the Lord's flock), condemning propositions specifically linked to a heresy that he called Modernism. Its philosophical basis was said to be situated in "agnosticism", Pius X's term for the immanentist principle that religion's source is human need, not God; from this fundamental mistake, the pope said, it follows that dogma "not only can but ought to be evolved and changed" and "all religions are true." No doubt it's correct, as critics have pointed out, that some of the propositions in *Lamentabili* were so vaguely worded that it is impossible to be sure what was being condemned. But the lasting significance of *Lamentabili* and *Pascendi* does not lie in their condemnation of particular propositions but in their rejection of the thrust of Modernist epistemology. Pope Pius lent his vigorous support in 1907 to a realist epistemology, against the relativizing, subjectivist theses propounded by the Modernists, which he termed agnosticism; as O'Connell remarks, "[H]e could hardly have spoken otherwise, unless he was prepared to jettison the whole of Catholic tradition." [45] Today,

---

is no positive truth in religion, but that one creed is as good as another, and this is the teaching which is gaining substance and force daily. It is inconsistent with any recognition of any religion as *true*. It teaches that all are to be tolerated, for all are matter of opinion. Revealed religion is not a truth, but a sentiment and a taste; not an objective fact, not miraculous; and it is the right of each individual to make it say just what strikes his fancy." Quoted in Ian Ker, *John Henry Newman* (New York: Oxford University Press, 1988), 721.

[45] O'Connell, *Critics*, 344. Another part of the Modernist package, closely related to those mentioned, was historicism. There is a good explanation of

some ideas associated with Modernism, especially in the area of Scripture study, are part of the orthodox Catholic consensus; but others are not, and indeed can never be.

An unfortunate offshoot of the Modernist affair was the launching, after the publication of *Pascendi*, of a campaign to neutralize anyone suspected of Modernist tendencies. Carried out under the direction of a Vatican official, Monsignor Umberto Benigni, this project involved a network of informers in dioceses who reported suspicious people to the authorities. In this way innumerable reputations and careers were harmed and scholarly work was stifled. Combined with other steps at the same time, the campaign created a chill in theological circles while, in the opinion of concerned observers, doing more to drive Modernism underground than to confront and correct it.

The heyday of Modernism in America, such as it was, occurred during the fifteen-year interval between 1895 and 1910. The American Modernists, not nearly as sophisticated as their European cousins, acted mainly as translators, commentators, and disseminators of the work of men like Loisy, Tyrrell, and von Hugel. The little band included a Notre Dame professor, Father John Zahm, who acquired a reputation as a writer on evolution and religion; William Laurence Sullivan, a Paulist, and John R. Slattery, a Josephite, both of whom ended up outside the Catholic Church (the "trajectory" of Modernism, according to Slattery, led inevitably to that result); faculty members at Saint Joseph's Seminary, Dunwoodie, in

---

it in Pope John Paul II's 1998 encyclical *Fides et ratio*: "The fundamental claim of historicism ... is that the truth of a philosophy is determined on the basis of its appropriateness to a certain period and a certain historical purpose. At least implicitly, therefore, the enduring validity of truth is denied" (*Fides et ratio*, 87).

Yonkers, New York; and the editors of the *New York Review* (some of the same people already mentioned), a short-lived journal that from 1905 to 1908 served as a vehicle for the propagation of Modernist thought. Pope Pius X's condemnation of Modernism effectively ended the nascent movement as a public phenomenon in the United States.

Modernism in America did not exist long enough for its links with Americanism to undergo extensive development. But links did exist. The American Modernists, says Appleby, were "influenced and encouraged by a generation of liberal churchmen, including the prelates John Ireland, John K. Keane, and John Lancaster Spalding, who called for the Roman Catholic Church in the United States to adapt itself to the values of the modern American republic". Ireland in 1893 could exclaim, "Church and Age! Unite them in the name of humanity, in the name of God." [46] The archbishop of Saint Paul failed to see the theological implications of Americanism, and later he rejected those of Modernism. [47] But others, like Zahm, saw the connections; and the understanding of Americanism and Modernism as "but two aspects of the same inchoate worldview"—a world view that "threatened to topple every traditional belief, including the efficacy of the sacraments, the supernatural character of the church, and the divinity of Christ"—was explicit in the writings of Sullivan and Slattery. [48]

Central to the vision of Americanists like Gibbons, Ireland, and Hecker was the conviction that Catholicism and

[46] Appleby, *Church and Age Unite!*, 86.

[47] "After Loisy left the pretention to orthodoxy behind in *Autour d'un petit livre*, Ireland realized with horror that he had helped spur a heretical movement." Ibid.

[48] See ibid., 7–10.

American culture were not simply compatible but complementary—an extraordinarily good fit, providentially designed
to assist the Catholic Church in her role as evangelizer of
the United States. More recently, some writers (e.g.,
Princeton's Stephen Macedo, Notre Dame's Jay Dolan) have
carried the argument further, maintaining that American
values and institutions have had, in Dolan's words, a profound influence on "the thinking of Catholics and the shape
of Catholicism's institutions", and this influence has been
on the whole for the good. In the end, Dolan concludes,
"Catholicism and American culture can indeed complement and enrich each other": "For two hundred years and
more, Catholics have been in search of an American Catholicism. This search will never end, but it is clear that at the
dawn of the twenty-first century, Catholicism is no longer
a stranger in the land. It has found a home in the United
States." [49]

That is one way to tell the story course. But there is
another way, of which Orestes Brownson is an early, exemplary figure. But not only Brownson—writing years later,
George Santayana, the erstwhile Harvard philosopher who
lived for most of forty years in the United States, marveled
at the readiness of Catholic immigrants to adapt so enthusiastically to an American culture that was deeply at odds
with their religious tradition.

> This faith . . . is full of large disillusions about this world
> and minute illusions about the other. It is ancient, meta-
> physical, poetic, elaborate, ascetic, autocratic, and intoler-
> ant. It confronts the boastful natural man, such as the
> American is, with a thousand denials and menaces. Every-
> thing in American life is at the antipodes to such a system.

[49] Dolan, *In Search*, 11.

Yet the American Catholic is entirely at peace. His tone in everything, even in religion, is cheerfully American. It is wonderful how silently, amicably, and happily he lives in a community whose spirit is profoundly hostile to that of his religion. . . . Attachment to his church in such a temper brings him into no serious conflict with his Protestant neighbours. They live and meet on common ground. Their respective religions pass among them for family matters, private and sacred, with no political implications.[50]

Today Francis Cardinal George, O.M.I., of Chicago, a past president of the Catholic bishops' conference of the United States and perhaps the most intellectual member of today's American hierarchy, strikes the same skeptical note as Brownson and Santayana.

What remains of the original Protestant ethos in contemporary American culture has been deformed into a secularized echo of Calvinism, particularly in the cultural emphasis on the notion of individuals determined by situations beyond their personal control, with the result that many perceive themselves to be victims. . . . As a result, the biblical message of freedom rooted in truth is treated at best as just one more personal option and at worst as a reactionary opposition to progressive cultural trends that are seen as liberating individuals from societal and institutional oppressions and dogmatisms of all sorts. . . . Society becomes a collection of individuals. Religious claims are at best private, and at worst morally oppressive.[51]

In saying such things, Cardinal George stands in opposition to larger-than-life predecessors like Gibbons and Ireland and

---

[50] George Santayana, *Character and Opinion in the United States* (London: Constable, 1924), 47–48.

[51] George, *Difference*, 85.

even to one of his own predecessors in Chicago, George Cardinal Mundelein, an ardent episcopal Americanizer in the middle decades of the twentieth century about whom we shall hear more in the next chapter.

Gibbons, Ireland, Mundelein, et al. may have been mostly right in their day, but their prescriptions for Americanizing Catholics and their Church are resoundingly wrong in ours. American culture has changed. Today's dominant secular culture is deeply hostile to Catholicism—in fact, to any religion that looks to divine revelation as a set of truths to be believed. Faithful Catholics, Orthodox Jews, and evangelical Protestants are therefore regarded as fair game by the secular powers-that-be, including the media. Continued uncritical Catholic assimilation into the surrounding culture is a destructive course for the Catholic identity of American Catholics. For those with eyes to see, Cardinal George suggests, the results already are clear. "The last forty years have seen a weakening of the Catholic Church's internal unity, because ecclesial renewal has been too often confused with secularization."[52] That doesn't mean dialogue between faith and culture in the United States should be halted (but it's fair to ask how much real dialogue is actually taking place). But it does mean the conversation, when and if it occurs, should be carried on "cautiously" by the Church, with an awareness of "inherent contradictions that were able to be overlooked in the enthusiasm of the 1960s and 1970s".[53]

In confronting the current situation, we also need to keep in mind another point made by Cardinal George—anyone who wants to reform and convert his culture must love it. That is essentially the same point Isaac Hecker made a

[52] Ibid., 83.
[53] Ibid.

century and a half ago. From an evangelical point of view, merely condemning American culture will accomplish nothing, however exhilarating that exercise may be for those who do the condemning. But the points at which the culture stands in irremediable conflict with Catholicism do need to be acknowledged and taken seriously.

As we shall see in the next chapter, during the twentieth century, developments in the relationship between Catholicism and American secular culture were dramatic and, in the end, notably alarming for the Church. The astonishing story of American Catholicism in the last century—a huge growth in numbers and power followed by a drastic contraction now verging on institutional collapse—can be likened to the voyage of a great ship that, rushing forward at full speed, strikes a submerged iceberg, comes to a shuddering halt, and slowly begins to sink. Captain, crew, and passengers face a difficult choice: man the lifeboats or stay with the vessel and work the pumps? One way or another, much of the rest of this book will be concerned with that particular question—the lifeboats or the pumps?—as it applies to the Catholic Church in the United States today.

On March 25, 1921, the *New York Herald* carried an editorial that read in part:

> The death of Cardinal Gibbons is more than the passing of an old man and honored churchman. It is the ending of the life of a great American, a fine figure in the national scene.
>
> In the sense that Francis of Assisi is everybody's saint, James Gibbons was everybody's Cardinal. No matter what their religious beliefs, Americans who knew him held him in the highest respect and esteem.

The *New York Times* agreed. Declaring that Gibbons possessed "the majesty of ecclesiastical, moral and intellectual authority", its editorial that same day pronounced him to be "one of the wisest men in the world". Many other voices were raised saying the same in one way or another.

James Cardinal Gibbons died on the morning of Holy Thursday, March 24, 1921, in his room in the rectory next to Baltimore's Assumption Cathedral, an edifice designed by the architect of the U.S. Capitol in Washington, D.C., Benjamin Latrobe. Gibbons was 86 and had been arch-bishop of Baltimore for 43 years.

The expressions of esteem and regret at his passing were not only very numerous but, it appears, unusually sincere. Here was a man who had been on friendly terms with every American president from Grover Cleveland to Wil-liam Howard Taft—a man admired by Catholics and non-Catholics alike, often consulted for his experience and good sense, respected in ecclesiastical circles in Rome as well as the United States. "Taking your life as a whole," his good friend Theodore Roosevelt had written Cardinal Gibbons in 1917, "I think you now occupy the position of being the most respected, and venerated, and useful citizen of our country." [54]

There is no reason to question his biographer's assessment:

[T]he failure to find brilliance of mind, depth of learning, mastery of administrative detail, resourceful and fighting qual-ities of leadership, powerful oratory, and majestic diction should not deceive one into believing that Cardinal Gib-bons was not a singularly gifted man. His gifts of prudence, discretion, and delicacy of perception were of an altogether uncommon order. . . . These gifts, resting upon a noble char-acter and implemented by a quick and agile mind, did more

[54] Quoted in Ellis, *Gibbons* 2:500.

than many others could have done who were far more richly
endowed than James Gibbons.[55]

And all these admirable gifts were placed consistently at the
service of Americanism.

It's sometimes supposed that Americanism had to do only
with the constitutional arrangements regarding religion and
government in the United States and their impact on the
Catholic Church. But for Cardinal Gibbons, Americanism
meant that and a great deal more.

A decade earlier, preaching in his historic cathedral on
October 1, 1911, on the occasion of a Mass celebrating the
golden jubilee of his ordination as a priest and his silver
jubilee as a cardinal, he shared his vaulting vision of America with the bishops and priests who had assembled to honor
him. "Your mission is to an enlightened American people
who are manly and generous, open to conviction, and who
will give you a patient hearing. The American race form
the highest type of a Christian nation when their natural
endowment of truth, justice and indomitable energy are
engrafted on the supernatural virtues of faith, hope and charity." No less exalted was his vision of an American Church—
bishops, priests, and laity "united in the cause of religion
and humanity".... "We form an impregnable phalanx which
cannot be pierced. We constitute a triple alliance far more
formidable and enduring than the alliance of kings and
potentates, for ours is not a confederation of flesh and blood,
but an alliance cemented by divine charity."[56] The legacy
that Gibbons wished to leave his Church and his nation
was everybody's cardinal's Americanist dream. American

[55] Ibid., 2:646.
[56] James Gibbons, "Jubilee Sermon Preached in the Baltimore Cathedral
on Sunday, October 1, 1911", in *Retrospect*, 2:143–44.

Catholics today, reflecting on their state of disarray, need to ask how far they are from realizing it, and why.

Here is a suggestion.

Part of the explanation may be that the Catholics of the United States have been preoccupied too long with the wrong question: What kind of Catholics should they be—"American" or "Roman"? But Catholicism itself is a given, open to only limited and rather well-defined variations without becoming something else. A better question for Catholics would be this: What kind of Americans do they want to be—assimilated creatures of the secular culture, or people of faith who seek for themselves a national identity superior to the one that the secular culture wishes to impose on them, an identity grounded in the gospel, leading them to distinguish carefully between what's acceptable and good in secular culture and what expresses secularist values in conflict with their faith?

As American Catholics, we are all heirs of the Gibbons Legacy. How we receive it and what we make of it are up to us. For a long time we've followed the Americanist prescription that calls for assimilation into secular culture, with hardly any questions asked. Perhaps that made sense in Gibbons' day, when the secular culture still expressed Christian values (but they were fading even then). Today, however, the results of doing that raise serious doubts about whether the Catholic Church in America, if she continues down this path, will continue to exist, even in her present diminished state of vitality. Here is the Gibbons Legacy now. American Catholics face no question more urgent than what they will choose to make of it from this point on.

2

INTO AND OUT OF THE GHETTO

It's 1916. Newly returned from studies in Rome and settling into his first pastoral assignment in a parish outside Boston, a young priest named Stephen Fermoyle sits at table in the rectory dining room, listening as the two senior curates debate matters of intense interest to him. Pope Pius X, dead now for two years, had published a motu proprio calling for the restoration of Gregorian chant. Father Lyons—"Milky"—thinks that's a great idea; Father Ireton does not, and he explains why.

"Pius X was a Patriarch of Venice.... No motorboats in the canals, no electric lights—just a lot of gondolas, singing boatmen, palaces on stilts, and all that. Fine. That's the tradition Pius X was working in. But now you get a man like our *pastoricus* here, a gadget-loving Westerner who doesn't know a square note from a round, living in an industrial town where electricity is cheap. Why in heaven's name should he prefer plain song to the nice ten-thousand-dollar electric organ he's just installed?"

"But plain singing is a heritage from the earliest Church," said Milky. "It has centuries of medieval tradition behind it."

"Plus three centuries of British—that is to say, Anglican—tradition," said Paul Ireton. "You wouldn't expect a man sprung from landlord shooters to embrace the practices of the landlord, would you?"

"You're being rather parochial," sniffed Milky.

"You mean," corrected Paul Ireton, "I'm being rather Boston-Irish."

Young Father Fermoyle is fascinated. On one side, there are the familiar parochialisms of the Irish-Americans that, being one of them himself, he knows so well; on the other side, "the universal viewpoint" he's acquired in Rome. "Could the two ever be fused?" he wonders. "Would America ever grasp the larger meaning of the Holy Roman Apostolic Church—an organization transcending national tongues, arts, and boundaries? And would Rome ever appreciate the peculiar vigor and quality of the transatlantic Church?" [1]

This scene occurs early in Henry Morton Robinson's novel *The Cardinal*. Published in 1950, the book sped to the top of the fiction best-seller list, beating out titles by writers like Ernest Hemingway and Frances Parkinson Keyes. *The Cardinal* finished no worse than fourth the following year, and in time was turned into a three-hour blockbuster movie directed by Otto Preminger. The question Stephen Fermoyle ponders there in the rectory dining room supplies a central theme of the book: Is it possible to be fully Catholic and fully American at one and the same time? Not surprisingly, Fermoyle's answer—and the answer of his creator, Henry Morton Robinson—is a resounding yes. I have no knowledge of whether Boston curates in the early years of the twentieth century were really in the habit of arguing about matters like these, but by the century's midpoint, when *The Cardinal* was published, Robinson's resounding yes was

[1] Henry Morton Robinson, *The Cardinal* (New York: Simon and Schuster, 1950), 54.

exactly what American Catholics wanted to hear—and what they wholeheartedly believed to be the case.

In many ways, the 1950s were the high-water mark for the Catholic Church in the United States up to this very day. The Church was growing in numbers, expanding rapidly in institutional presence and strength, becoming a powerful cultural force. But success, as so often, came at a price—in this case, increasing suspicion, indeed outright hostility, toward Catholicism in key sectors of American society, reminiscent of, but far more sophisticated than, the old anti-Catholicism of the past.

Just a year before *The Cardinal* was published, Paul Blanshard, a lawyer and writer for the liberal magazine the *Nation*, had published a best seller of his own called *American Freedom and Catholic Power*. Blanshard posed essentially the same question Stephen Fermoyle asked: Could good Catholics be good Americans? His answer was a resounding no, and he was far from being alone in that. According to historian John T. McGreevy, American liberalism by now was committed to the proposition that "religion, as an entirely private matter, must be separated from the state, and that religious loyalties must not threaten intellectual autonomy or national unity".[2] Catholicism was held suspect on all of these counts.

In the *Everson* case of 1947, the Supreme Court began its labor—which was to continue into the 1970s—of raising a "wall" of absolute separation between church and state; during oral arguments on *Everson*, Justice William O. Douglas passed a note to Justice Hugo Black, who was to write the majority opinion, reading, "If the Catholics get public money to finance their religious schools, we better insist on getting

[2] John T. McGreevy, *Catholicism and American Freedom* (New York: Norton, 2003), 168.

some good prayers in public schools or we Protestants are out of business." [3] Other members of the Supreme Court voiced similar views reflecting an animus against the Catholic Church.[4]

It was in this climate of opinion that *The Cardinal* made its appearance. The novel is a long, sprawling book whose story covers the dramatically charged years from 1915 to 1939. Hundreds of characters, lofty and lowly, admirable and despicable, swarm through its 500-plus pages. It isn't great literature, but it's eminently readable and immensely helpful to anyone seeking to understand the mind of American Catholicism at its midcentury apex, at once triumphalistic yet curiously defensive and unsure of itself, like a new boy at school miming self-confidence that he doesn't entirely feel.

At the heart of the story stand Stephen Fermoyle and Lawrence Cardinal Glennon, the crusty, autocratic archbishop of Boston, who becomes the younger man's patron, friend, and father figure. The Fermoyle-Glennon relationship depicted in the book was widely understood to be a highly idealized version of the relationship that really had existed between William Cardinal O'Connell of Boston and Francis Cardinal Spellman of New York during the penitential years of the latter as O'Connell's unsought, unwanted auxiliary bishop from 1932 to 1939.

It's easy to understand the tension between these two highly ambitious churchmen. As a student in Rome and, later, rector of the American College there, O'Connell had made highly placed friends in the Vatican through whom he won appointment to the hierarchy and eventually to the post of archbishop of Boston. But this was no easy thing.

---

[3] Ibid., 185.

[4] On the attitude toward Catholicism of various members of the Supreme Court at this time, see ibid., 183–88.

An intense power struggle preceded O'Connell's transfer in 1906 from the small diocese of Portland, Maine, to the giant archdiocese of Boston. This contest pitted an Americanist faction led by Archbishop Ireland of Saint Paul against conservatives headed by Archbishop Corrigan of New York (though he was dead by 1906), with these old antagonists lobbying for their candidates. Nor was O'Connell shy about promoting his own cause, at one point warning the Vatican secretary of state that his opponents could be counted on to oppose "any name which stood for Rome. . . . Boston is at this moment in the balance between Rome and her enemies." [5]

The conservatives won, O'Connell went to Boston, and, in the words of a chronicler of these events, "the door slammed shut on the Americanists." [6] True to his promises, O'Connell became the leading Romanist in the American hierarchy of his day. But his notable success in gaining admission to the exclusive social circles of non-Catholic Boston along with significant political influence placed him in the front ranks of the Catholic struggle for entry into the American mainstream—"the beneficiary and avatar of the American Catholic belief that it was possible to be fully loyal to the pope and fully loyal to one's own country at the same time".[7]

Not surprisingly, then, when the young and upwardly mobile Francis Spellman arrived on the scene a quarter century after the older's man's accession, Cardinal O'Connell regarded him as an ambitious upstart whose up-to-date Roman connections—notably including Spellman's good friend Eugenio Cardinal Pacelli, now the secretary of

[5] James M. O'Toole, "The Name That Stood for Rome: William O'Connell and the Modern Episcopal Style", in *Patterns of Episcopal Leadership*, ed. Gerald P. Fogarty, S.J. (New York: Macmillan, 1989), 177.

[6] Ibid.

[7] Ibid., 184.

state—were better than his own. Clipping Spellman's wings was O'Connell's objective during the seven unhappy years he spent before Pacelli, now Pope Pius XII, promoted Spellman to New York just two months after becoming pope.

But the subject here isn't personalities and politics at the upper reaches of the hierarchy, interesting as the matters may be. By the early 1900s, thanks to *Testem benevolentiae*, Americanism and the Americanists had indeed had the door slammed shut on them, and their setback in Boston was one more confirmation of that. Yet the process of Americanization continued, although in ways slower and subtler than someone like John Ireland might have liked. We return now to that story as it continued to play itself out.

The first four decades of the century brought the flowering of ethnic identity as a central principle of American Catholicism, and ethnicity now was to play an important, complex role in Catholic assimilation. The process was neither simple nor trouble free, as events in Chicago in the early 1920s soon made clear.

> It is of the utmost importance to our American nation that the nationalities gathered in the United States should gradually amalgamate and fuse into one homogeneous people and, without losing the best traits of their race, become imbued with the one harmonious national thought, sentiment and spirit, which is to be the very soul of the nation. This is the idea of Americanization. This idea has been so strongly developed during the late war that anything opposed to it would be considered as bordering on treason.[8]

[8] Quoted in Jay P. Dolan, *In Search of an American Catholicism: A History of Religion and Culture in Tension* (New York: Oxford University Press, 2002), 139–40.

This manifesto of the melting pot is part of a rebuttal dispatched to the Vatican on behalf of the American bishops in reply to an impassioned 13-page letter from Polish priests ministering to Polish Catholics in Chicago and elsewhere in the United States. The priests' letter denounced George Cardinal Mundelein of Chicago and his brother bishops for blocking the efforts of Polish immigrants to keep and assert their ethnic cultural identity—of which Polish-style Catholicism was a key part—in the new country. Indeed, they claimed, Cardinal Mundelein and bishops like him were "intent upon the destruction of their nationality".[9] The cardinal and the bishops were equally blunt in their rebuttal to the Holy See: "It will be a disaster for the Catholic Church in the United States if it were ever to become known that the Polish Catholics are determined to preserve their Polish nationality and that there is among the clergy and leaders a pronounced movement of Polonization."[10]

Apparently agreeing with Mundelein and the bishops, the Vatican took no action on the priests' plea. But although the Polish Catholics had lost in Rome, they were to win in Chicago.

The background of this struggle mirrors an old story that we've already seen at work in the nineteenth century in the case of German-American Catholics. Like the Germans, the Poles felt they were getting short shrift from the powers-that-be of the Church in America. And they had a point. In Chicago, where Poles made up more than half the city's Catholics, Cardinal Mundelein set his face against the "hyphenated American" and declared integration to be his goal. Abandoning previous archdiocesan policy of

[9] Quoted in ibid., 139.
[10] Quoted in ibid., 140.

encouraging nonterritorial parishes for particular nationality groups, Mundelein assigned Polish priests to non-
Polish parishes, took steps to make the archdiocesan seminary
an "engine of Americanization", and mandated the use of
English as the language of instruction in parochial schools.[11]

The Polish priests, angry and dismayed, turned to the
Polish government and sought its intervention with Rome.
The Polish legation to the Holy See submitted the priests'
petition to the Vatican secretary of state. He in turn sent it
on to Cardinal Gibbons for the American bishops' consid-
eration. The bishops then established a committee of three,
with Cardinal Mundelein one of them, who prepared the
acerbic rebuttal quoted above. And, not surprisingly, at the
official level, that was the end of the matter.

But Chicago's Poles persisted, and in the end it was the
cardinal who had to back down. The practice of assigning
Polish priests to non-Polish parishes was halted; the number of Polish parishes and Polish parochial schools continued to grow. Cardinal Mundelein's fundamental mistake, it
appears, had been to attempt to separate religion and culture for the sake of hastening Americanization. Whatever
else might be said of it, where the Polish Catholics of Chicago were concerned, that policy was premature in the 1920s.
(It was no less unrealistic, one might add, to adopt a similar
approach to the growing number of members of Eastern
Catholic Churches in union with Rome, who in these years
waged a continuing struggle with the American hierarchy
and the Holy See to be allowed to retain their own identity
and customs within the framework of the overwhelmingly
Latin Church in the United States.)

[11] For an account of these events, see e.g., Jay P. Dolan, *In Search of an American Catholicism*, 138–41; Dolores Ann Liptak, R.S.M., *Immigrants and Their Church*
(New York: Macmillan, 1989), 114–30.

Immigration was the spur that drove these conflicts. From 1865 to 1925 immigration brought 25 million newcomers to America, and very many of these were Catholics. Changes in American immigration law eventually reduced the torrent to a trickle, but already by 1920 the Catholic population in the United States totaled 18 million. At least 75% of that number belonged to one or another of the 28 distinct ethnic groups that made up the body of American Catholicism, with the largest of them the Irish, the Germans, Italians, Poles, French Canadians, and Mexicans.

This ethnic diversity naturally was reflected in ecclesiastical structures, especially the growing number of national parishes established to serve the pastoral needs of language groups. Even today it's easy to find cities and towns, especially in the eastern states and the Midwest, where several Catholic churches—the "Irish church", the "Italian church", the "Ukrainian church", and so on—are located within the same few square blocks, relics of an era eight or more decades ago when ethnic Catholicism was a vital force in the life of these communities. Jay Dolan describes the multidimensional significance of such religious enclaves:

> These were community institutions that Catholics established to preserve the religious life of the old country. They were also social institutions that strengthened the social fabric of the community by nurturing families as well as faith and by promoting education as well as Sunday Mass. By organizing their national parishes, immigrant Catholics hoped to hear sermons in their mother tongue, practice the devotions and customs of the old country, and raise their children in the faith of their fathers and mothers.[12]

[12] Dolan, *In Search of an American Catholicism*, 91.

But, Dolan adds, the flowering of ethnic Catholicism raised an unavoidable question in some minds: "Would Catholicism in the United States be a church of foreigners or would it become an American church?"[13]

National parishes and the celebration of ethnicity they represented are often described as central elements of the "Catholic ghetto" as it existed in the first half of the twentieth century. The term is more pejorative than the reality it refers to deserves. This distinctively Catholic subculture served, among other things, as a useful halfway house shielding newcomers to America against the shock of too-rapid assimilation by allowing them to celebrate their hyphenated Catholic identity while simultaneously honing newly acquired American cultural skills.

Catholics living in this so-called ghetto lived, worked, shopped, and in time intermarried with nonhyphenated Americans. They scrimped to send their children to colleges and universities with other American kids. They read the same papers (along with foreign-language papers, to be sure), listened to the same radio shows, went to the same movies, and rooted for the same teams as everybody else. The ghetto metaphor suggests a far more radical state of cultural isolation than existed in fact. The Catholic Americanizers have used it, one suspects, at least partly to further their own political ends.

Still, the question—"A church of foreigners or an American church?"—did get asked, and often by enemies of the Church. As the cultural tide of Catholicism rose, nativist anti-Catholicism rose along with it. In *The Cardinal*, this hostility from the outside is offered as an explanation for

[13] Ibid., 92–93.

certain well-known patterns of behavior existing within the Church. Stephen Fermoyle's first pastor is an Irishman named Monaghan whose devotion to the Sunday collection has earned him the nickname "Dollar Bill". Father Monaghan is no figment of the author's imagination. Even now, Catholics of a certain age can recall hearing "green sermons" preached with some regularity at Sunday Mass: the point thus driven home was that the preacher didn't want to hear the irritating clatter of coins falling into the collection basket but only the soft, soothing flutter of bills. Henry Morton Robinson explains how Dollar Bill Monaghan got that way:

> As a youth he had felt hunger to the marrow of his large leg bones; but even more painfully he had felt the hatred and contempt in which his unpropertied kind, the South Boston Irish, were held by Boston Brahmins. . . . If Father Monaghan overvalued property, it was because the society in which he lived overvalued it, too. Ownership of something—that was the badge of membership. . . . A well-constructed church of Quincy granite or a prosperous parochial school of fine brick was an outward sign of substance that could not be blown down or whirled about by winds of prejudice.[14]

One episode in the novel focuses on the ill-fated Al Smith campaign of 1928. Recalling the real-life role of the famous Father Francis Patrick Duffy, chaplain of New York's "Fighting 69th" Regiment in World War I and a close friend of Smith, the ubiquitous Fermoyle has a brief role as an adviser to Smith, whose campaign as Democratic candidate for president was running into a brick wall of virulent anti-Catholicism.

Smith probably would have lost to Republican Herbert Hoover in any case; politically speaking, the pre-Depression

---

[14] Robinson, *Cardinal*, 44.

boom years of the 1920s belonged to the GOP. But bigotry contributed to the size of Smith's defeat, which saw Hoover winning 58.2% of the popular vote and 444 electoral college votes to the New Yorker's 40.77% and 87. Two months before the election, a Protestant magazine sounded what by then had become a familiar note, declaring that "the mere mention of a Roman Catholic as President" was cause for alarm. "Today", remarked the editorial writer, "Rome has reached one of its long-sought goals. It well behooves us to emphasize before our people those cardinal principles which came forth as fruit of the Reformation, on which our government is founded.... Rome has not changed.... Eternal vigilance is the price of liberty." [15]

That sort of rhetoric stung, and the bitterness lingered for years in the hearts of many Catholics. Recalling the events of 1928, *The Cardinal* more than two decades later attributed to its high-minded hero these angry sentiments in the face of "scalding injustice":

> How long would these men persist in regarding the Church as a band of conspirators plotting against the Constitution? Would such men never realize that Catholicism in the United States was a cornerstone of civil order, a bulwark against the corrupting forces of anarchy and decay? To those who accused the Church of undermining American freedom, Stephen wanted to cry out: "Our sole aim is to inculcate patriotism founded upon divine law. Our only objective is to help men keep alive the light of their souls, the hope of heaven, the love of God." [16]

---

[15] In *American Lutheran*, September 1928, quoted in George J. Marlin, *The American Catholic Voter: 200 Years of Political Impact* (South Bend, Ind.: St. Augustine's Press, 2004), 185.

[16] Robinson, *Cardinal*, 405.

Long after 1928, such sentiments were still being transmitted from pulpits, in parochial school classrooms and Knights of Columbus meeting halls, and in the pages of the Catholic press. One long-term result of Al Smith's defeat was thus to mobilize Catholics as a national political force and help set the stage for a run at the White House more than thirty years later by a Catholic named John F. Kennedy.

The Cardinal can be read as a kind of hymn to the ethnic Catholicism of the Boston Irish in the years from World War I to World War II. Henry Morton Robinson saw the warts of the Irish subculture, but he was captivated by its charms. Others, looking at the same phenomenon, found little to celebrate—on the one hand love, on the other loathing.

James T. Farrell falls on the side of loathing. Farrell's *Studs Lonigan* trilogy is a brutal, naturalistic account of Irish Catholicism in Chicago as the author experienced it in the same years covered in Robinson's novel. For Farrell, this is a cramped, bigoted, soul-destroying world.

A high point of the trilogy's third volume, *The Young Manhood of Studs Lonigan*, is a sermon preached in the late 1920s by a mission priest in Lonigan's parish, Saint Patrick's.

"Missions" were (still are, in fact, although they're much less common in American Catholicism now than used to be the case) periods of intense devotional activity in which a visiting priest or priests labored to revive the dormant religious fervor of the people of a parish. In Farrell's version, Father Shannon's harangue, directed to the young people of an overwhelmingly Irish-American parish, falls short of the famous sermon by a Jesuit retreat master in James Joyce's *Portrait of the Artist as a Young Man*, but in its own right it's a highly effective, even compelling, caricature.

After warning his listeners—at length—against the evils of illicit sex ("You don't want to disease your body so that a decent person will shun you as a leper")[17] and drink, the priest ("plump, bald-headed" with a "soft, mushy, almost womanly face") winds up like this:

> It is you, your kind, your class, to which America looks. And if America is to avoid that drastic, terrible fate which befell the proud and mighty empire of Rome, it is you, and others like you, who will have achieved the victory. I can't save America. My generation cannot. But yours can. That is why Mother Church counts on you. She knows that today she must fight one of the greatest battles she has ever fought. She faces a world where materialism drives out the laws and will of God and Nature, where sin is rampant, where money is poured into the coffers of vice, making it rich and powerful, where great industries are built up only to pander to lust, where books, theatres, movies, universities, are all aligned on the side of godlessness, and where all these forces together constitute a mighty propagandistic effort to take her sons and daughters from her and give them into the hands of Satan. And her fight is your fight.[18]

Farrell apparently means this as mockery, but he misses the underlying nobility of its naïve message of patriotic, albeit unappreciated, service to a nation gravely imperiled by its own moral weakness, which not even Farrell's contempt can wholly erase. This simplistic but heartfelt vision of moral uplift on behalf of America was still another current in the broad stream of the Americanist impulse as it still flowed in the "ghetto" Catholicism of the twentieth century.

[17] James T. Farrell, *The Young Manhood of Studs Lonigan*, in *Studs Lonigan* (New York: Signet Books, 1958), 394.

[18] Ibid., 395–96.

American Catholicism of this era also embodied a form of conspicuous clericalism in which the clergy ruled while the laity looked on with mingled awe, admiration, and irreverence.

Awe and admiration are laid on with a heavy hand in *The Cardinal*'s account of Fermoyle's ordination as bishop of a fictitious diocese called Hartfield that bears a striking resemblance to Hartford, Connecticut. It begins like this:

> At ten o'clock that morning, while four thousand worshipers knelt inside the Cathedral and an exterior multitude clogged traffic on Athenaeum Avenue, a procession of richly vested clerics, preceded by cross-bearer, acolytes, and choristers, entered the center door of the great church. A full organ swelled jubilantly into *Ecce sacerdos magnus*.... The ecclesiastical train approached the altar. Soon the sanctuary was a pool of crimson and gold; throughout the Cathedral softer blocks of color marked the presence of religious orders: Carmelites and Dominicans in white, Paulists in black, Capuchins in coarse brown.... Dennis and Celia Fermoyle scarcely dared lift their eyes to the solemn pageant in which their son was playing the central role.[19]

And so on and on, a clericalist festival is described in loving detail to the very end of the lengthy ritual. Then, as Bishop Fermoyle strides up the aisle and gives his parents his blessing, the two old people put their heads together like "dumb creatures ... sharing knowledge not communicable to others".

As for irreverence, an incident from my days at Georgetown in the mid-1950s may serve to illustrate its presence in an oddly sublimated form.

Inspired by I know not what mischievous spirit of rebellion, I'd written a short story about a priest who quits the

[19] Robinson, *Cardinal*, 378.

priesthood, marries, and now makes a living denouncing the Catholic Church, and had turned it over for publication to the college literary magazine. I felt no misgivings, since I'd made it clear that I considered this behavior by an ordained minister of the Catholic Church to be highly reprehensible. As I was soon to find out, though, that wasn't good enough. Learning at the last minute what was going on, the *Journal*'s faculty adviser, a nontenured assistant professor of English and a tolerant, friendly man, abruptly laid down the law: Absolutely not! Under no circumstances could that story about an ex-priest appear in the Georgetown *Journal*.

Censorship was bad enough, but I was told to go see a Jesuit priest high up in the university administration—to be lectured on my sins, I supposed. I was embarrassed, but Father X, to my surprise, was apologetic—concerned not with chewing me out but, decent chap that he was, with offering me an explanation for the censorship to which he apparently hoped I would assent. I had to understand, he told me, that if my story were published, Georgetown parents and alumni might see it. But this wasn't what they expected to read in the literary magazine of a respectable Catholic school. *They* would be upset, and Georgetown couldn't afford to have that happen, could it? I *did* see the point, did I not?

After more of the same, Father X finally let me go. I was relieved. I think he was too. "Thank you, Father", I mumbled. I didn't know it at the time, but he'd done me a favor. My story, pompous, moralistic, and obtuse like its author, was a truly dreadful piece of work, though mild by comparison with the far stronger stuff that one day was to bedevil the Church.

But where was the clericalism in all this? Not in the suppression of a young writer's inferior story. Had it been published, it might well have dogged me for years ("Oh, you're the one who wrote that story about the priest . . ."). If the Jesuit had merely said, "It's a bad piece of writing that doesn't meet Georgetown's standards", I'd have had to agree, if not then, certainly now. And neither then nor now could I quarrel with Father X's rationale, considered as statement of fact: "Parents and alumni would be upset." Some really might have been upset if they'd bothered to read the piece.

That, however, is the point. Even in the 1950s, most adult Catholics were at least dimly aware that, along with many priests who persevered, there were some who defected from the ranks of the ordained. But this was a reality many preferred not to recognize, opting instead for the clericalist myth that all priests lived up to the demands of their high calling (some better than others, of course). Graham Greene and Georges Bernanos already had written about priests beset by human weakness, and had been criticized in some ecclesiastical quarters for doing that. But I was no Greene or Bernanos, and my story, though it condemned defections from the priesthood, nevertheless violated the rules of the clericalized Catholic subculture of that day by requiring readers—specifically, Georgetown parents and alumni who might happen to encounter the story—to face a fact they preferred to ignore.

A trivial incident, to be sure. Yet perhaps not so trivial in its larger implications. Not so many years later, it was just this habit of denial among the laity that would make its own contribution to the hierarchical cover-up of clergy sex abuse by supplying part of the rationale for suppressing disagreeable facts: "Our people would be scandalized if they knew." In the Catholic clericalist world of *The Cardinal*, neither the book's author nor, apparently, anyone else saw anything odd about likening the parents of the story's priest-hero, in his hour of triumph, to "dumb creatures".

Clericalism in the Catholic Church has a long history and deep roots; I've written about it elsewhere at length.[20] In the United States, it took on a special edge from the controversy over lay trusteeism (lay ownership and control of parishes) that preoccupied the American bishops for much of the nineteenth century, making virtually any lay initiative more or less suspect as a result. For example, when Henry F. Brownson, Orestes Brownson's son, suggested holding a lay congress in November 1889 to mark the centenary of the American hierarchy, Cardinal Gibbons expressed "considerable misgiving" and agreed to the proposal only on the condition that a committee of bishops review in advance the papers to be presented at the gathering; even so, Gibbons declined an invitation to attend.[21]

The situation of the laity started to change in the early decades of the twentieth century with the emergence of the movement called Catholic Action. It had the ardent support of Pope Pius XI—"the pope of Catholic Action"—and other Church leaders, who saw it as a way of restoring the Church's influence in the secular order (sadly reduced by anticlerical calamities like the French Revolution and the Italian Risorgimento) through the use of loyal laypeople as a body of apostolic shock troops. Michael Cardinal von Faulhaber (1869–1952), the anti-Nazi archbishop of Munich, supplied a good, brief explanation of the theological rationale underlying Catholic Action: "By Baptism we

---

[20] For example, *To Hunt, To Shoot, To Entertain: Clericalism and the Catholic Laity* (San Francisco: Ignatius Press, 1993).

[21] John Tracy Ellis, *The Life of James Cardinal Gibbons, Archbishop of Baltimore, 1834–1921* (Milwaukee: Bruce, 1952), 1:413–15.

have been elected building stones in the structure of the kingdom of God; having received Confirmation we are called, as builders, to lay other stones in the structure of this kingdom.... [W]e are not only to be fishes in the net of the Apostles, but are ourselves to be fishers of men and Apostles." The cardinal nevertheless was careful to add that the pope had "clearly and precisely defined Catholic Action as 'participation of the laity in the hierarchical Apostolate.' "[22]

The flowering of Catholic Action in the United States in the 1920s, 1930s, and 1940s found visible expression in the rise of organizations and movements devoted to forming laypeople to engage the structures of secular society in order to evangelize them. Here was Isaac Hecker's program brought up-to-date. Besides a school system extending from the elementary grades to graduate and professional schools, the network of programs acting on the Catholic Action model included groups directed to Catholic students, workingmen, academics, lawyers, physicians, nurses, and pharmacists, along with persons engaged in many other professions and pursuits.

When the midcentury shift away from the Catholic ghetto began, the organizational elements of this infrastructure fell into disfavor with Catholic intellectuals who saw them as vestiges of an immature Catholicism (as very likely they were to some extent) and instead pressed for the unmediated integration of Catholics into the secular milieu. A

---

[22] Michael Faulhaber, "The Essential Characteristics of Catholic Action", in *Readings for Catholic Action*, ed. Burton Confrey (Manchester, N.H.: Magnificat Press, 1937), 14. The Second Vatican Council (1962–1965) was to endorse the idea of an autonomous lay apostolate, carried on both individually and collectively. Strange to say, the postconciliar innovation known as lay ministry, though frequently hailed as a breakthrough for the laity, is a retreat to the pre–Vatican II Catholic Action model, with functions formerly restricted to the clergy now open to laypeople to perform under clerical supervision and control.

student of these events calls the demolition of the old infrastructure that rapidly ensued "organizational *hara-kiri*" and
concludes that "without an effective and authentic mode
of Catholic mediation, the dominant and now secular mainstream culture has had an almost uncontested ability to shape
the minds and hearts of the younger generations of American Catholics."[23]

But that's getting ahead of the story.

Along with being clericalized, American Catholicism of
this era was triumphalistic. The message of triumphalism
was clear and, often enough in those days before Catholic
entry into the ecumenical movement, bluntly stated: the
Catholic Church possesses the truth; therefore, she is invari-
ably right, and people who refuse to recognize these self-
evident facts must be blinded by ignorance or bigotry or,
quite possibly, both.

Often the truth claims were backed up by symbolic dis-
plays of muscle, the most notable of these being the Twenty-
Eighth International Eucharistic Congress held in Chicago
July 20–24, 1926. This was the first of these mammoth public exhibitions of Catholic devotionalism in the United States,
and the congress of 1926 mirrored Cardinal Mundelein's
determination to show the world that Midwestern Catholicism on the Chicago model was now a force to be reck-
oned with.

Churchmen from around the world attended, joining a
throng of ordinary faithful in Soldier Field on the shores of
Lake Michigan for a busy program of liturgies and talks.
The final day brought the pièce de résistance: an outdoor
Eucharistic procession by a crowd variously estimated at

[23] Joseph A. Varacalli, *The Catholic Experience in America* (Westport, Conn.:
Greenwood Press, 2006), 46.

800,000 and 1 million at the archdiocesan seminary, Saint Mary of the Lake, which Cardinal Mundelein had built on a heroic scale on a rolling thousand-acre campus beside a lake twenty miles outside the city. (The nearby town was renamed Mundelein in 1924.)

Chicago's Catholic newspaper, the *New World*, disclaimed triumphalistic intent in all this: "Let there be no mistaking the fact that the Eucharistic Congress is no endeavor to demonstrate strength. There is no thought behind it of a flaunting of vast numbers before non-Catholics." [24] Perhaps. It is hard to believe, though, that Cardinal Mundelein and his associates weren't aware that vast numbers were being flaunted or that they felt very bad about the flaunting. A historian remarks: "Such triumphal display may seem like megalomania, but it was more than personal vainglory. Mundelein was trying to carry a whole institution—a whole generation of immigrant outsiders—upward with him. Acutely aware that Catholics in America lacked self-confidence and social status, he tried to burnish the image of the Catholic church." [25] This same project—bolstering Catholic self-esteem and wowing non-Catholics—was also being pursued at that time by Cardinal O'Connell in Boston, Cardinal Dougherty in Philadelphia, and other leaders of the Church in America.

Self-conscious image burnishing didn't disappear quickly from American Catholicism, though in time it did undergo mutations of a sometimes bizarre sort. On August 30, 1957,

---

[24] Quoted in Edward R. Kantowicz, "The Beginning and the End of an Era: George William Mundelein and John Patrick Cody in Chicago", *Patterns of Episcopal Leadership*, ed. Gerald. P. Fogarty (New York: Macmillan, 1989), 206.

[25] Ibid.

Cardinal Spellman of New York celebrated the twenty-fifth anniversary of his ordination as a bishop in a ceremony in Yankee Stadium.

> The apostolic delegate, four cardinals, eighteen archbishops, eighty-three bishops, and two abbots were on hand, along with thousands of cheering well-wishers. A large procession of uniformed police and firemen, members of the Holy Names [*sic*] societies, opened the ceremonies by marching from the left field bullpen onto the baseball field, which featured a huge raised platform dominated by an immense cross. Then Spellman made a grand entrance from right field, escorted by twenty West Point cadets in full-dress uniform. He was clad in gold robes trimmed in scarlet; even his miter was gold with scarlet trim. The St. Joseph's Seminary choir, stationed behind home plate, sang "Behold the Great Priest." [26]

No one knew it then, but the cardinal's anniversary celebration was a last fling. In little more than a year, the Church would see the death of Pope Pius XII and the election of Pope John XXIII, events that set in motion currents that within a few short years were to render such triumphalistic exhibitionism obsolete in many places and make it an object of criticism and disdain wherever it lingered.

As the showy use of military academy cadets in a quasi-liturgical role at the Spellman anniversary suggests, [27] American Catholicism in these years clung to the same

[26] Thomas C. Reeves, *America's Bishop: The Life and Times of Fulton J. Sheen* (San Francisco: Encounter Books, 2001), 255.

[27] It is only fair to point out that Cardinal Spellman, besides being archbishop of New York, was in charge of the military ordinariate serving the spiritual needs of Catholics in the armed forces. Since then the ordinariate has been replaced by a military archdiocese whose archbishop does not wear two hats.

hyperpatriotism celebrated by Americanists like John Ireland in the nineteenth century. As a Catholic variety of American exceptionalism—America in the familiar role of city on a hill, a providentially supplied norm and model for other nations and peoples—this mentality served as a natural, protective response on the part of members of a religious minority aware that they were widely viewed as interlopers and anxious to show themselves just as American as, and perhaps even *more* American than, anybody else. In April 1917, a day before Congress declared war on Germany, thus plunging America into World War I, Cardinal Gibbons had issued a statement to the press in which he said in part: "The primary duty of a citizen is loyalty to country. This loyalty is manifested more by acts than by words; by solemn service rather than by empty declaration. It is exhibited by an absolute and unreserved obedience to his country's call." [28]

In its Catholic form, however, nationalism had another dimension that pointed to a continuing struggle in Catholics' minds and hearts to reconcile their religious and their civic identities—to persuade *themselves* not only that they were fully American but that to be American and to be Catholic were complementary and mutually reinforcing of being who they truly were. Shrewdly perceiving this to be the great unresolved issue at the heart of the Catholic experience in America from colonial times to his own day, Henry Morton Robinson returned to it repeatedly at key moments in his wildly popular novel—as in the following.

The year is 1926. A new apostolic delegate—Stephen Fermoyle's old professor and friend, Archbishop Alfeo Quarenghi—has just arrived in the United States and is being feted at an intimate gathering of clerical heavyweights

---

[28] Statement of April 5, 1917, in Ellis, *Gibbons*, 2:239.

in the residence of the archbishop of New York just behind
Saint Patrick's Cathedral. After dinner, the group adjourns
to the study, and there Quarenghi takes the floor. Striding
to a huge map of the world that flanks the fireplace,

> the Apostolic Delegate now laid his open palm on the shield-
> shaped curvature of the United States; seemingly he expe-
> rienced the tactile pleasure of a man rubbing a ruddy apple.
> "This is the land I have so often envisioned in fancy. What
> may we not expect from a country so boundlessly blessed
> by God? I speak not of the iron in your hills, the carbon in
> your mines, the torrential power generated by your rivers
> and machines. I speak rather of the spirit generated by your
> people—the spirit of American fortitude and resourceful-
> ness, tinged by an almost mystical trust in its own destiny." [29]

Here is what Fermoyle/Robinson takes to be "the intu-
itional scope of the Roman mind", engaged now in tracing
"a vast migration toward a divine goal". But what goal is
that? Nothing less than the recognition and total acceptance by American Catholics of "their responsibility to the
future". The apostolic delegate goes on: "I come neither as
a meddler nor an overseer [precisely those activities of a
papal legate that Americanists like Gibbons and Ireland had
so feared half a century earlier], but merely to remind you
that the world looks to the Catholics of the United States
for a rekindling of the spiritual flame that is now almost
extinguished in the world. If your light fails, there is dan-
ger of universal darkness." [30]

It's a speech worthy of Isaac Hecker himself. And bear in
mind that, although in the novel set in 1926—the eve of

---

[29] Robinson, *Cardinal*, 345.
[30] Ibid., 345–46.

the portentous and disaster-laden 1930s—it appears in a book that was published in 1950, in a postwar United States painfully facing up to the realities of cold war waged against an implacable, officially atheistic adversary committed by ideology to world domination.

The point—Catholicized America has a divine mission to save the world—becomes still clearer at the close of the book. Now it's 1939. Fermoyle, a cardinal by then, is sailing home from Europe after the conclave at which his friend Eugenio Cardinal Pacelli has become Pope Pius XII. Fermoyle has a special assignment from the new pope as a top-level liaison between the Holy See and the American government (a role that Cardinal Spellman to some extent actually played[31]).

World War II is imminent. Out on the North Atlantic one night, Cardinal Fermoyle is deep in meditation as his British liner threads gingerly through a field of towering icebergs. The symbolism is clear: Western civilization (British ocean liner) is menaced by deadly threats from the North (Nazi Germany, Stalinist Russia—*The Cardinal*, after all, was written from a postwar perspective). But not to worry. A prince of the Church stands in the bow of the noble vessel, seeing all, understanding all, and praying the great ship and its passengers home to safe haven—the embrace of the world's greatest democracy, deeply infused with the wisdom of the holy, catholic, apostolic Church of Rome.

"Vigilance, wrought of hope and faith, would bring the vessel through", Cardinal Fermoyle reflects.[32]

As they'd done in every other American war, U.S. Catholics in large numbers fought in World War II. The Church

---

[31] See Gerald P. Fogarty, S.J., "Francis J. Spellman: American and Roman", in Fogarty, *Patterns*, 216–34.

[32] Robinson, *Cardinal*, 512.

vigorously supported the war effort. The habits of hyper-patriotism, combined with a more general Catholic tendency in the direction of uncritical support of political authority, may help account for the fact that Catholics, like Americans generally, raised no objections to the use of atomic bombs at Hiroshima and Nagasaki.

True, a friend recalls being told by a nun who was a parochial schoolteacher at the time that she and other teachers received a written communication from the pastor telling them they were welcome to tell their students that deliberately bombing civilians was wrong. But this seems to have been an exception. Certainly there was no general Catholic outcry against the use of the bomb. On the contrary, my reaction as a ten-year-old Catholic—that the "Japs" had picked this fight at Pearl Harbor and deserved whatever they got, and besides, the new weapon had saved many *American* lives by bringing the war to a speedy close—probably mirrored that of most of the Catholic adults around me.

One of the few Catholics who protested was the leading American moral theologian of the day, John C. Ford, S.J. Father Ford is remembered now as a leader of the minority on the papal birth control commission who supported the Church's constant teaching on contraception before Pope Paul VI's encyclical *Humanae vitae* of 1968. But that was to come later. In 1944, in the journal *Theological Studies*, Ford published a 49-page article arguing against the killing of the innocent by the obliteration bombing of cities that was then being carried out by the American and British air forces.[33] A year later, in his "Notes on Moral Theology" in the same journal, having acknowledged the atrocities

[33] John C. Ford, "Morality of Obliteration Bombing", *Theological Studies* 5 (1944): 272.

committed by the Soviets, the Nazis, and the Japanese, he nevertheless spoke of "the greatest and most extensive single atrocity of all this period, our atomic bombing of Hiroshima and Nagasaki".[34]

The words were widely noted in theological circles, but they didn't reach me or most other American Catholics at the time. Even now, it appears they haven't reached many.

On the eve of World War II, Nazism and Fascism were the great objects of American fear and loathing. Soon after the war, however, communism took its place in the national psyche. Here was a switch Catholics had little intellectual or spiritual difficulty making, having been schooled in militant anticommunism for years. With deliberate intent, Pope Pius XI's anti-Nazi encyclical *Mit brennender Sorge* and his anticommunist encyclical *Divini redemptoris* were published less than a week apart in March 1937: two peas from the same pod was Pius XI's message regarding both totalitarian systems. American Catholics entertained no illusions about either. True, during the 1936–1939 civil war in Spain, most Catholics had backed the Fascist-tinged forces of General Franco, but who would have expected anything else? After all, the anarchists, communists, and others on the Republican side of that bloody struggle had executed 12 bishops, 283 religious sisters, 4,184 priests, and 2,365 religious men, most of them in the war's early days.[35]

[34] John C. Ford, "Notes on Moral Theology, 1945", *Theological Studies* 6 (1945): 540.

[35] British historian Michael Burleigh calls this killing of clergy and religious "the largest example of anticlerical violence in modern history", surpassing even the French Revolution; see Burleigh's *Sacred Causes* (New York, HarperCollins, 2007), 131–32. American Catholics can hardly be blamed for not entertaining warm feelings toward its perpetrators.

Catholics were among the first and most vociferous groups to oppose communism in the United States. Anticommunism meshed easily with their existing religious and patriotic loyalties, since militant atheistic Marxism was understood as a threat to both their country and their Church, whose interests were very nearly identical in any case.

One of the earliest and most eloquent American Catholic anticommunists was Monsignor Fulton J. Sheen, a philosophy professor at the Catholic University of America, a prolific author, and, in the pretelevision days of the 1930s, a nationally famous radio preacher whose "Catholic Hour" listening audience rivaled that of the increasingly strident and problematic radio priest Father Charles Coughlin.

Speaking to an audience of 43,000 in a stadium in Cleveland in 1935, the charismatic Sheen sounded an apocalyptic note. "In the future there will be only two great capitals in the world, Rome and Moscow; only two temples, the Kremlin and St. Peters; only two tabernacles, the Red Square and the Eucharist; only two hosts, the rotted body of Lenin and the Christ Emmanuel; only two hymns, the Internationale and the Panis Angelicus—but there will be only one victory—if Christ wins, we win, and Christ cannot lose." [36] The linkage of anticommunism, Americanism, and Catholicism in Sheen's world view became ever clearer as American entry into World War II approached. By then, the infamous Hitler-Stalin pact of 1939 had dissolved, and Hitler had invaded Russia. Speaking in Brooklyn in November of 1941, Sheen said the Nazi leader sought "to crush Russia, not communism. He would destroy Christianity all over the world if he

[36] Quoted in Reeves, *America's Bishop*, 100.

could." [37] But that didn't make the Soviet Union a friend of the United States, since if communism were to emerge victorious from the war, "America's problems would be just beginning." [38]

Recalling the spirit of that era, a friend of mine notes that as a student at a parochial school in Queens, New York, he and his classmates, returning from recess on the playground, "marched up the stairs to the tune of 'Stars and Stripes Forever', 'The Marine Hymn', and the Notre Dame fight song". After years of such tutelage by Sheen and many other sources in the Church, including the mainstream Catholic press, it was only natural in the early Cold War years that Catholics, including the leadership of the Church, should welcome the efforts of one of their own, Senator Joseph McCarthy of Wisconsin, to expose communist agents supposedly entrenched in sensitive positions in government and the military. Communist spying was a fact—consider Alger Hiss—but McCarthy's carelessness about facts eventually led to his downfall. Cardinal Spellman nevertheless supported him publicly and, in a generous pastoral gesture, continued to extend private acts of personal kindness to the Catholic senator's family until near the end. Even so, it was not until the years of the Vietnam War two decades later that the hyperpatriotism of American Catholicism grounded in anticommunism splintered.

Considered in this light, it is easy to understand the popularity enjoyed in the 1950s by a populist apostolic movement called the Christophers, which combined opposition to communism with a form of generically Christian witness that, downplaying doctrinal and denominational

[37] Ibid., 145.
[38] Ibid., 146.

differences, sought to bring religious values to bear in every-day life. A historian writes of the group's founder, Father James Keller, M.M.: "Keller argued that from the perspective of the communists, America and religion were the two greatest enemies; no distinction need be made between Catholics and Protestants. At the crossroads of civilization, people should come together in an unselfish offensive against paganism." [39] His program provided a synthesis of patriotism and faith that offered American Catholics an answer, broadly appealing at the time, to the old challenge of harmonizing the tenets of the American sociopolitical arrangement, which they eagerly embraced, with their religiosity.

One must be cautious in speaking of the spiritual lives of American Catholics during the half century before Vatican Council II. God reads souls; people who write books don't—although some may be tempted to imagine otherwise. Bearing this fundamental truth in mind, however, a few generalizations are in order.

Obviously there were many good, even holy, American Catholics in this era. "Renewal" was not required for grace to flow through the channels that the Church provided—the Mass and the sacraments; sacramentals like the rosary; devotions like the First Friday observance linked to the Sacred Heart, benediction of the Blessed Sacrament, Forty Hours, and Corpus Christi processions; retreats and parish missions; individual and corporate prayer; and the support of foreign missions and charitable programs and institutions dedicated to spreading the gospel and relieving human misery.

---

[39] Joseph P. Chinnici, O.F.M., *Living Stones: The History and Structure of Catholic Spiritual Life in the United States* (New York: Macmillan, 1989), 201.

Indeed, American Catholicism as a whole was an impressive picture of success in those years. Vocations to the priesthood and religious life were booming; parochial schools were crowded; with the Catholic population near 25 million, the rate of Sunday Mass attendance in the 1940s was 75%; long lines of Catholics waited outside confessionals every Saturday to confess their sins to the priest and have them forgiven by God, and in the 1950s and early 1960s over 80% of Catholics went to confession yearly or more often. Sometimes it's said that numbers like these were then at a historically atypical high point, and perhaps they were. But at the time they also reflected a brilliant pastoral achievement in making real the norm of Catholic participation in the life of their Church.

With the advantage of hindsight, however, it's now apparent that along with its good qualities American Catholicism in the age of *The Cardinal* suffered from such bad ones as triumphalism, clericalism, and legalism. For many Catholics, practicing the faith was largely a matter of external observance: Mass on Sunday, fish on Friday, making their Easter duty (confession and Communion once a year), marrying in the Church, not practicing birth control or at least confessing it if they did. Vatican II's universal call to holiness had yet to be sounded, much less heard.

Among those who sensed that something was wrong with all this was Dorothy Day. After living a bohemian life as a writer and journalist, Day converted to Catholicism in 1927. In 1933 she and a Frenchman named Peter Maurin founded the Catholic Worker, a movement devoted to preaching and living a radical form of Catholicism focused on identification with the poor. While never large in numbers, the Catholic Worker had a significant impact on many Catholic intellectuals of a religiously serious turn of mind, clergy and laity alike, who found its intensity and authenticity a relief from the superficiality of mainstream Catholicism and enthusiastically responded to its message of solidarity with poor people, pacifism, and spiritual idealism.

What Day found in the mainstream American Catholicism of those times was not encouraging. In her autobiography, she speaks of her feelings soon after her conversion.

> I loved the Church for Christ made visible. Not for itself, because it was so often a scandal to me. . . . The scandal of businesslike priests, of collective wealth, lack of a sense of responsibility for the poor, the worker, the Negro, the Mexican, the Filipino, and even the oppression of these, and the consenting to the oppression of them by our industrialist-capitalist order—these made me feel often that the priests were more like Cain than Abel. . . . The worst enemies would be those of our own household, Christ had warned us.[40]

Writing 21 years after the fact, Day also conceded that since that time she'd gotten to know many priests who were "poor, chaste and obedient, who gave their lives daily for their fellows", but this, she added, was "how I felt at the time of my baptism".[41] The Catholic Worker was founded at least in part in reaction to this perception of the Church and her leaders.

One member of the clergy who lived up to Dorothy Day's expectations was a Pittsburgh priest named John Hugo. Though little known then and largely forgotten now, Father Hugo in the 1930s, 1940s, and 1950s enjoyed a certain fame in advanced Catholic circles as Day's spiritual director and a preacher of retreats and writer. Criticized as a rigorist and

---

[40] Dorothy Day, *The Long Loneliness: The Autobiography of Dorothy Day* (Garden City, N.Y.: Image Books, 1959), 145–46.

[41] Ibid., 146.

"Jansenist" and ostracized by fellow priests, he was ordered by his bishop not to give retreats and was exiled to a rural parish until a later bishop rehabilitated him. Having been vindicated by Vatican II's emphasis on the idea that all members of the Church without exception are called to personal holiness, he continued preaching and writing—often in defense of the Catholic sexual ethic now challenged by dissenters within the Church—until his death in a car crash in 1985. Among the fairly small number of American Catholics of this era with a strong, distinctive ascetical message, the Trappist monk Thomas Merton is by far better known, but John Hugo has more to speak to our present subject; rather than viewing and judging his Catholic contemporaries from the isolated vantage point of a monastery, Hugo rubbed shoulders with the human reality of the Church as a parish priest, hearing confessions, giving pastoral counsel, and interacting with the ordinary faithful.

Already in the 1940s he was conscious, and critical, of the "confident assimilation" of American Catholics into the larger American culture that World War II and postwar developments had spurred, and had come to believe that its most serious result was "a watering down of Catholic identity" that turned these assimilated Catholics away from distinctively Catholic beliefs and rituals while asking little of them beyond observing minimal middle-class standards of behavior. The editors of a collection of his writings recall that Father Hugo "called this bland creed 'pious naturalism' or, more severely, 'paganism,' a betrayal of Christ and His saving message".[42]

---

[42] David Scott and Mike Aquilina, eds., *Weapons of the Spirit: Selected Writings of Father John Hugo* (Huntington, Ind.: Our Sunday Visitor Publishing Division, 1997), 17.

Even among those Catholics who were "wholly faithful to the external obligations of religion", the priest observed bitterly in a privately circulated manuscript written in 1947, "large areas of their lives are wholly unilluminated by their faith.... [T]hey are indistinguishable from the huge sickly mass of paganism which surrounds them." Birth control, then "making headway among Catholics", was a case in point.

> Economic pressure is alleged. This may be at least the occasion for sin among poor families, hence the just indignation of men against those priests who thunder against birth control while being themselves very comfortable in the social conditions that make birth control appear to many as a necessity.
>
> Economic pressure however does not explain the prevalence of this sin among the prosperous—worldliness does. Those who commit it balance the law of God over against the advantages to be gained through birth control—unrestrained pleasure, physical beauty, leisure, freedom from the responsibility of a family, the opportunity to use all one's income on luxuries, and the satisfaction of earthly ambitions.
>
> For the vast majority of our Catholic people it is possible to combine with a blameless *notional* or speculative assent to the chief mysteries of the faith a multitude of diminutions and evasions in the practical mind.[43]

It seems likely that John Hugo would be no more popular today than he was then.

Father Hugo may have been a rigorist. Dorothy Day was an idealist. Both may have been unfair in their judgment of American Catholicism as they found it. But considering all

[43] Ibid., 95.

that's happened since then, they appear to have been dead right.

In 1950, when *The Cardinal* was published, the Catholic Church in the United States was at a higher peak of success than she had ever reached before or has reached since. American Catholicism—awkward and unsure of itself it was, but like an adolescent bursting with vitality and newfound strength—wanted only an opportunity to test how strong it had become. A few years earlier, the influential Protestant magazine *Christian Century* had published a widely noted series of eight articles under the general title "Can Catholicism Win America?" *Christian Century* concluded that it could, and, as if channeling Isaac Hecker, many Catholics seemed to agree.[44] Summing up the achievements of Philadelphia Catholicism in the glory days of Dennis Cardinal Dougherty, who reigned in autocratic splendor in the City of Brotherly Love from 1918 to 1951, and taking the Church of Philadelphia as representative of the Church in America, historian Charles R. Morris concludes that American Catholicism at this time was "slowly becoming the dominant cultural institution in the country".[45] But even though hardly anyone guessed it, the whirlwind of cultural change was now at hand.

Henry Morton Robinson and *The Cardinal* provide a useful vade mecum to the mind of American Catholicism up to the middle years of the twentieth century. Another book—a long journal article, really, though soon published between covers—provides a helpful introduction to the

---

[44] Harold Fey, ed., *Christian Century*, "Can Catholicism Win America?", November 29, 1944–January 17, 1945.

[45] Charles R. Morris, *American Catholic: The Saints and Sinners Who Built America's Most Powerful Church* (New York: Times Books, 1997), 195.

cultural revolution that swept American Catholicism in the
years immediately following 1950.

American Catholics and the Intellectual Life is the work of
the ubiquitous historian, biographer of Cardinal Gibbons,
and commentator on all things Catholic: Monsignor John
Tracy Ellis.[46] My introduction to this sensational exercise
in Catholic self-laceration came just shortly after it first
appeared. It was late 1955 or early 1956, and I was sitting
with 30 or 40 other seniors in a cavernous classroom on
the second or third floor of Georgetown's White-Gravenor
Hall, waiting for philosophy class to begin. (Thirty or 40
students may seem a rather large number for a class presumably devoted to serious reflection on great ideas, but in
those years philosophy was a required subject for juniors
and seniors in Georgetown's College of Arts and Sciences,
and the university powers-that-be had determined in their
wisdom to cope with the large numbers that resulted by
clustering students in big classes that the harried professors
taught by lecturing.)

A minute or two before the hour, Professor "McThomas" (not his real name) hurried in and took his place on
the platform at the front of the classroom, prepared to address
us. A youngish, lantern-jawed layman, McThomas was the
sort of transparently earnest teacher that even a coldhearted
undergraduate finds it hard not to like. He gave every appearance of taking his subject seriously and, against all odds, of
being truly desirous of sharing the glories of neo-Thomism
with his generally unappreciative students. In fact, he was
one of my better teachers. That day, though, he had something besides neo-Thomism on his mind. Laying aside

---

[46] John Tracy Ellis, *American Catholics and the Intellectual Life* (Chicago:
Heritage Foundation, 1956).

textbook and notes, McThomas spoke fervently about something he'd just read.

After so many years, I don't recall exactly what he said, but I do remember the subject—John Tracy Ellis' piece on Catholics and the intellectual life, only recently published in a Fordham University journal called *Thought* (it has long since vanished) after having been delivered earlier as a lecture to a group called the Catholic Commission on Intellectual and Cultural Affairs. Dr. McThomas found Tracy Ellis' article enormously exciting, and in his estimation so should we students. Truth to tell, I doubt that many of his listeners that day did; I surely didn't. But if I drew nothing else from his words, at least they made me aware that this Catholic academic whom I liked and respected had found enlightenment and inspiration—and, very likely, confirmation—in what Tracy Ellis had said.

It was only years later that I sat down and read the piece. Its fundamental message is simple: American Catholics, in proportion to their numbers, were making a woefully inadequate contribution to the nation's intellectual scene, and this failure was "the weakest aspect of the Church in this country".[47] There were several explanations for that: anti-Catholicism, which had caused Catholic writers to concentrate on apologetics rather than on "pure scholarship"; the material and intellectual disadvantages of being a Church of immigrants; the overall tradition of American anti-intellectualism, together with the specific lack of an American Catholic intellectual tradition; and others as well.

The failure of American Catholicism to render significant service to the intellectual life, Monsignor Ellis forcefully argued, was fully reflected in the failures of American

[47] Ibid., 16.

Catholic colleges and universities. With relish he quoted a 1937 address by Robert M. Hutchins, president of the University of Chicago, delivered at a regional meeting of the National Catholic Educational Association. The Catholic Church, Hutchins had said, possessed "the longest intellectual tradition of any institution in the contemporary world"; yet Catholic higher education in the United States had "imitated the worst features of secular education and ignored most of the good ones".[48] Ellis entirely agreed with that, while also adding his own specifically religious note to the indictment of Catholic schools: "the absence of a sense of dedication to an intellectual apostolate".[49]

In conclusion, the historian held that the "chief blame" for this sorry state of affairs rested with Catholics themselves: "It lies in their frequently self-imposed ghetto mentality which prevents them from mingling as they should with their non-Catholic colleagues, and in their lack of industry and the habits of work.... It lies in their failure to have measured up to their responsibilities to the incomparable tradition of Catholic learning." [50]

Strong stuff. Then and now, some thought Tracy Ellis had laid it on too thick. For even as he wrote, it was said, American Catholic colleges and universities on the whole were not so bad, some were quite good, and many were on the way to getting better as a result of reforms undertaken even before Monsignor Ellis spoke up.

I leave this argument to others. In late 1955 and early 1956 it was clear that Monsignor Ellis' critique evoked passionate assent among Catholic members of the academy

---

[48] Quoted in ibid., 43.
[49] Ibid., 45.
[50] Ibid., 57.

like Professor McThomas. *American Catholics and the Intellectual Life* had delivered the right message at the right time to an audience more than ready to hear it.[51]

Looking back, it's easy to see that many faculty members in these schools, like my philosophy professor, carried a heavy burden of chagrin arising from the perceived inferiority of the schools where they taught—an inferiority that, as they saw it, rubbed off on them and made it hard to publish in professional journals and climb the academic ladder in the circles to which they craved admission. This situation, which they deeply resented, made them internal critics of their own schools, a discontented academic proletariat agitating for change. The following story of the Gold Key Society illustrates that.

In my years as an undergraduate at Georgetown, this venerable Jesuit-run school, the oldest Catholic university in the United States, occupied an ambiguous position in American higher education. A buttoned-down school controlled and tightly run by the Society of Jesus (all of the top administrators were Jesuits, and many Jesuits were faculty members), Georgetown made Mass attendance mandatory for Catholic resident students and enforced a curfew in its all-male dorms. Possessing alcoholic beverages in a dorm room was a crime punishable by expulsion. In the unisex College of Arts and Sciences, the study of Latin was required for

[51] Two years after the incident recalled here, a newcomer to the Georgetown philosophy department found Dr. McThomas still enthusiastic about the Ellis piece. The newcomer, with a doctorate from a major American secular university, was more reserved. He argued that Monsignor Ellis was mistaken insofar as he evaluated Catholic higher education by secular standards; the real problem with Catholic higher education was that instead of effectively promoting Catholic intellectual life, it was busy catering to a well-to-do clientele. Dr. McThomas naturally disagreed with that.

liberal arts majors during the first two years, while much of the junior and senior years was given over to courses in neo-Thomistic philosophy. Theology was a required course all four years. Georgetown had a reputation as "a Catholic Ivy League school", but it was not clear just what that meant. Most obviously, it signified that a good number of the students came from well-off, even wealthy, families and dressed in an ostentatiously preppy manner. Beyond the Catholic ghetto, however, the academic rank of the Hilltop (as Georgetown was called) was problematic.

For those with eyes to see, one sign of that was the absence of a Georgetown chapter of Phi Beta Kappa, the national academic honor society. I don't recall ever hearing the Phi Beta Kappa problem discussed, but I have no doubt now that discussions did take place, probably heated ones, among at least some of the faculty and administration. Georgetown wasn't alone, of course. A 1958 study found that of 23 Catholic schools applying for Phi Beta Kappa chapters between 1931 and that year, only two—the College of Saint Catherine and Fordham—had been granted them. Institutions like Georgetown and Notre Dame were conspicuously out in the cold. Some people blamed this on anti-Catholicism, others on the academic weakness of the Catholic schools. Probably both factors were at work.

Georgetown's solution was to create a kind of in-house Phi Beta Kappa—an honor society of its own that would recognize distinguished achievement without seeking a stamp of approval from Phi Beta Kappa or any other outside source. It was called the Gold Key Society. Membership, exclusively at the invitation of the university, was advertised in the catalogue in glowing terms as the highest academic honor Georgetown could bestow on undergraduates.

One day—I suppose it was during my junior year—I stopped outside the office of the dean of the College of Arts and Sciences to scan the notices posted on the bulletin board. One of them announced new members of the Gold Key Society. Among the several names listed was mine. My heart swelled with pride. I'd scaled the heights of Olympus! With eager anticipation I looked forward to the splendid festivities that surely would accompany the bestowal of this singular event.

I waited in vain. There were no splendid festivities. That anonymous notice on a bulletin board was the only thing that marked my elevation to the Gold Key Society. No induction ceremony. No letter of commendation. In fact—no Gold Key. Nobody said a word about it. I waited and waited, but nothing happened. Georgetown had given me its highest undergraduate academic honor, and as far as I could see, Georgetown couldn't care less.

I found this baffling then, but now I think I understand. Somewhere along the line, Georgetown had stopped believing in the Gold Key Society. The formality of naming new members was still observed (perhaps carried out as a mechanical task by a secretary in the dean's office who checked grade point averages). But no faculty member or member of the administration took it seriously. Phi Beta Kappa was what mattered, and, much to its embarrassment, Georgetown didn't have that. No wonder John Tracy Ellis' polemic excited Professor McThomas. Here was the path to academic excellence as it was understood in the academic world beyond the Hilltop and the campuses of other Catholic schools. This was the way Georgetown would have to go.

And it did. Years later, thanks to the efforts of a friendly English professor who remembered me from the old days, I was grandfathered into the recently established George-town chapter of Phi Beta Kappa, joining a group of cheer-ful young men and women who received this honor along with me. The Gold Key Society was gone. And gone too was Professor McThomas, who'd left Georgetown for what I hope were greener academic pastures. That was a loss, but one my old school could afford, being by now well on its way to recognition as one of the nation's elite academic institutions.

In a prefatory note to *American Catholics and the Intellectual Life*, Bishop John J. Wright of Worcester, Massachusetts (later bishop of Pittsburgh and later still cardinal-prefect of the Vatican's Congregation for the Clergy) wrote that Monsignor Ellis had made "an unusually important contribution to the interpretation and, perhaps, even the direction of our times on the relationship of Catholicism to American intellectual life".[52] Indeed he had. The out-pouring of books, articles, and speeches that followed Ellis' indictment, hammering away at the Church's colleges and universities and demanding change, was a clear indication that the eminent historian had spoken, force-fully and publicly, what others had thought, but seldom said, for years. Although neither Bishop Wright nor any-body else could have known it at the time, the Catholic colleges and universities had taken their initial steps down the path that would lead a dozen years later to Land O' Lakes—the nickname for the 1967 manifesto in which rep-resentatives of the nation's leading Catholic schools would assert their institutions' autonomy in relation to the Church's Magisterium. We shall see more about that in the next chapter.

[52] John J. Wright, "Prefatory Note", in Ellis, *American Catholics*, 5.

Predictably, Georgetown was swept along in this powerful current blending change and conformity. And now? Successful, probably beyond the wildest dreams of Professor McThomas and others like him in my undergraduate days, Georgetown is regularly ranked among the top universities in the nation.

That has come at a price. How high a price was suggested by an evaluation published by the conservative ecumenical journal *First Things* in one of those college-ranking features popular with magazines. Calling Georgetown a "poster child for post-Catholic higher education", it concedes that the university has some teachers "committed to the Catholic mission in higher education". But they are exceptions in a faculty said generally to be "hostile to Catholicism", and the school has "a culture that pulls students away from their faith". In these circumstances, the university's administrators are obliged to attempt an impossible balancing act, between "appeasing the often anti-Catholic faculty and gentling the Catholic alumni while marketing to Catholic parents of potential students".[53]

It is not a happy situation, *First Things* concludes; and although the picture of Georgetown thus painted is perhaps a bit exaggerated, other observers see it much the same way. And not just Georgetown but the many other schools— "post-Catholic" in *First Things'* phrase—whose commitment to Catholic identity is shaky at best.

Life in the Catholic subculture in the middle years of the twentieth century is vividly described by Kenneth L. Woodward, former religion editor of *Newsweek*. Growing up in a

---

[53] "Degrees of Faith: A *First Things* Survey of America's Colleges and Universities", *First Things*, November 2010.

parish in a Cleveland suburb and, above all, attending Catholic schools, provided, he writes, "an initiation into a vast parallel culture". To be sure, other religious groups had subcultures of their own. "But at mid-century only Catholics inhabited a parallel culture that, by virtue of their numbers, ethnic diversity, wide geographical distribution, and complex of institutions, mirrored the outside 'public' culture yet was manifestly different.... Catholic education was the key.... [T]he religious identity we acquired in childhood was a primal identity that absorbed and conditioned all the others." [54] The story of this subculture's collapse has been told many times[55] and needn't be repeated in detail here. What happened was generally along the following lines.

After the war, military veterans in large numbers took advantage of the G.I. Bill to attend college at government expense. Many were Catholics, often the first members of their families to get a college degree. More education meant better jobs and higher pay. In due course, these upwardly mobile veterans married, started families, and, now earning comfortable salaries, bought homes in the new suburbs to accommodate the four- and five-child families that were typical in those baby-boom years. The movement of these Catholics to the suburbs had the inevitable result of draining the old inner-city ethnic parishes and neighborhoods of people and vitality, while the advantages of suburban living usually failed to include a strong sense of community and a religious identity centered on church and parochial school.

[54] Kenneth L. Woodward, "Memories of a Catholic Boyhood", *First Things*, April 2011.

[55] See, for example, Joseph A. Varacalli, *Bright Promise, Failed Community: Catholics and the American Public Order* (Lanham, Md.: Lexington Books, 2000), 55–58 and passim, and Morris, *American Catholic*, vii–ix and passim.

Up to this time, as Joseph Varacalli points out, American Catholicism's vitality had been based largely on the fact that the faith was "embedded in a Catholic cultural milieu and set of institutional arrangements that surrounded the Catholic individual in his/her round of daily existence, hence constantly reinforcing and reasserting the reality and imperatives of that faith".[56] Now, for young Catholic families scrambling to make it in the sprawling, religiously and ethnically pluralistic suburbs of post–World War II America, that no longer was the case.

It would be a mistake, though, to see the breakdown of the Catholic subculture as something that simply happened, with no one intending it or working to bring it about. On the contrary, important elements of the Catholic intellectual and leadership classes deliberately worked to accomplish this result.

John Tracy Ellis had deplored what he saw as the "pervading spirit of separatism from their fellow citizens of other religious faiths" that he believed existed among Catholics generally and Catholic intellectuals in particular. "They have suffered from the timidity that characterizes minority groups, from the effects of a ghetto they have themselves fostered. . . . The chief blame, I firmly believe, lies with Catholics themselves. It lies in their frequently self-imposed ghetto mentality."[57] The indictment resonated with others who

---

[56] Varacalli, *Catholic Experience*, 33.

[57] Ellis, *American Catholics*, 56–57. Monsignor Ellis had a point. For example, a pamphlet called *The Power and Apostolate of Catholic Literature*, apparently aimed at Catholic high school students and issued by a Jesuit-operated publishing house called the Queen's Work in 1938, lists members of something called the Gallery of Living Catholic Authors situated at Webster College in Missouri. The American laureates in this group said to constitute "the top of the list of Catholic writers" include such names as Leonard Feeney, S.J.; James Gillis, C.S.P.; Monsignor Peter Guilday; Daniel A. Lord, S.J.; and

took up the hue and cry against the ghetto and the ghetto mentality that were supposedly impeding Catholic assimilation into American culture, and soon this theme became a familiar cliché of Catholic books and articles of the era. The effect was what Varacalli terms "a pervasive 'secularization from within'".[58]

Besides railing against the ghetto, the critics worked to destroy it, often with the cooperation, active or passive, of ecclesiastical leadership. This process of what was thought to be the tearing down of ghetto walls occurred not only in Catholic higher education but also within the laboriously constructed infrastructure of Catholic organizations and movements that had grown up in the 1920s, 1930s, and 1940s, particularly under the inspiration of Catholic Action, as the fruit of the program laid out for the Church in America by the hierarchy's Baltimore Councils in the nineteenth century. By the late 1950s, says Charles Morris, as the social assimilation of Catholics that opponents of Americanism had viewed with alarm 60 years before forged ahead, "parallel Catholic professional organizations, like Catholic medical societies and teachers' guilds, began to be abandoned by their members, or to play down their Catholic affiliation." (In a typical instance of that, the *American Catholic Sociological Review* became *Sociological Analysis*.)[59] Other Catholic periodicals and groups moved in the same direction.

It is important to repeat that at the time, destroying the ghetto seemed a good idea. The *Catholic Almanac*s of the

---

Sister M. Madeleva, C.S.C. All worthy individuals, no doubt; but only in a cultural ghetto would they be offered as models for emulation by aspiring young writers. It is interesting that Webster College a few years later was one of the first American Catholic schools to secularize itself.

[58] Varacalli, *Bright Promise*, 5.
[59] Morris, *American Catholic*, 277.

1940s and 1950s were, a friend points out, "perfect examples of insular Catholic culture, with Catholic baseball statistics and lists of Catholics elected to office. Why would a Catholic want or need to buy any other almanac, as it might include information about Protestants and other inappropriate reading materials?"

But like many another project launched under the influence of ideology and strong feelings, the dismantling of the Catholic subculture and its plausibility structure had unintended, and sometimes unpleasant, consequences. "When I was growing up," the same friend recalls, "I watched the Legion of Mary and other local Catholic organizations struggling for lack of interest on the part of the priests and chancery office staff, who saw them as anachronisms. Even as a young man, I could note the sadness and the frustration in the faces of many older members, especially as nothing was being offered as a replacement or as a new form of devotion."

While today's descendants of the Americanists appear reluctant to acknowledge consequences such as these, that isn't the case with writers like Varacalli and Morris. According to Varacalli, the Church's plausibility structure has been so "battered and defiled" since the 1950s and 1960s "and hence so weakened in its ability to provide an alternative worldview considered attractive and compelling"—that the Church in the United States now suffers from a drastically reduced capability to evangelize either Catholics or non-Catholics.[60] Morris calls the destruction of the so-called ghetto a "fearsome exercise" in cultural demolition—nothing less than "the dangerous and potentially catastrophic project of severing the connection between the Catholic religion and the

---

[60] Varacalli, *Catholic Experience*, 68.

separatist American Catholic culture that had always been the source of its dynamism, its appeal, and its power".[61]

As an intellectual project, the Americanization of American Catholicism reached a peak of sorts in the work of John Courtney Murray, S.J. For most people, Murray today may be best remembered as the Jesuit who made the cover of *Time* magazine and for having helped bring about the affirmation of religious liberty in the teaching of the Second Vatican Council, but his larger goal was to situate a significant part of the Catholic intellectual tradition—natural law—at the heart of American public life.

In his book *We Hold These Truths*, published in 1960 on the eve of Vatican II, Murray in a way picked up where *The Cardinal* had left off ten years earlier, arguing the case for Catholic thought as a central source, and now a providentially intended defender, of the democratic institutions of the United States and the West against the totalitarian threat of Soviet communism. But Murray, in arguing that Catholicism was by right at home in the heart of America, was far more sophisticated than comparatively simplistic precursors like the founders of the Knights of Columbus or Henry Morton Robinson had been; and rather than propose that institutional Catholicism now directly assume its rightful place in American culture, he sought to have it render its beneficent service to the nation through the instrument of natural law.

Granted, Murray wrote, it was true that "its [natural law's] dynamic had run out" at this moment in history, so that its "impotence" as a solver of social problems was clearly

[61] Morris, *American Catholic*, 279–80.

"demonstrable".[62] Still, convinced of the perennial value of
the natural law tradition, Murray was no less convinced that
its revival and renewal were not only necessary but possible. What he could not have anticipated was the imminent
repudiation and collapse of the tradition, not only in secular circles but also in Catholic academe. In a few short
years, caught up in the swirling currents that accompanied
Vatican II, Murray's beloved natural law tradition had been
all but swept away. Whether everywhere and forever, only
time will tell.

Then came the Council and, after the Council, something
very nearly resembling anarchy.

In four momentous autumn sessions from 1962 to 1965,
the fathers of Vatican Council II hammered out a consensus that can today be found in the 103,000 Latin words of
its four constitutions, nine decrees, and three declarations.
Among the myths about Vatican II is the idea that that it
was a strictly "pastoral" council, without significant new
doctrinal content. In fact, the Council produced a sizable
body of important teaching, which can be found in its six-
teen documents.

Extreme traditionalists, led by Archbishop Marcel Lefebvre, dug in to resist, while on the far left "progressives"
hungered for more change than the Council had delivered. When Lefebvre ordained new bishops without the
pope's permission, he and his bishops were excommunicated and the Lefebvrist movement entered into a de facto
state of schism. Meanwhile, the progressives had com-
plaints of their own. "The renewal of the Catholic Church

---

[62] John Courtney Murray, S.J., *We Hold These Truths: Catholic Reflections on the American Proposition* (New York: Sheed and Ward, 1960), 301.

and ecumenical understanding with other Christian churches
... had got stuck", says Father Hans Kung, the Swiss-
born theologian who in this new era became a kind of
prince of dissenters and something like a counterpope.[63]
The supposed corruption of the Church often supplied
grounds for dissent. Charles Davis, a prominent British theologian who quit the priesthood in 1966, spoke for more
than just himself in declaring his "revulsion" regarding the
"Roman claims" of the pope.[64]

The largest building block of this new Catholic culture
of dissent was the "spirit of Vatican II". In the United States,
this spirit was born immediately after the Council, with
special thanks to Xavier Rynne and other progressive Catholics. "Rynne" was the pseudonym of an American Redemptorist priest, Francis X. Murphy, who, while the Council
was on, authored a series of insider reports in the *New Yorker*
depicting Vatican II as a titanic struggle pitting heroic lib-
erals against dastardly conservatives, with the Church's future
course at stake. Soon after the Council, he and his like-
minded associates began arguing that more important than
the Church documents was the fact that it had inaugurated
a new era of continuing, open-ended change in Catholicism.

French Thomist philosopher Jacques Maritain, a resident
of the United States, also saw a new spirit at work in the
Church but was not happy with it, and gave what he considered its characteristic posture a provocative name: "kneel-
ing before the world". In *The Peasant of the Garonne*, first
published in France in 1966, just a year after Vatican II ended,
he deplored what he found to be a widespread abandonment

---

[63] In Hans Kung, *The Catholic Church: A Short History* (New York: Modern Library, 2003), 187.

[64] Quoted in George A. Kelly, *The Battle for the American Church* (Garden
City, N.Y.: Image, 1981), 316.

of values like asceticism, mortification, and penance, along with virginity and chastity, and their replacement by a simpleminded immanentism. Maritain cited the case of a homilist who rendered Saint Paul's "a thorn was given me in the flesh, an angel of Satan to harass me" (2 Cor 12:7) as "I am having trouble with my health." Of such foes of the tradition he wrote:

> [T]he great concern and the only thing that matters for them is the temporal vocation of the human race, with its march, embattled but victorious, to justice, peace, and happiness. Instead of realizing that our devotion to the temporal task must be that much firmer and more ardent since we know that the human race will never succeed on this earth in delivering itself completely from evil . . . they make of these earthly goals the truly supreme end for humanity.[65]

In other words, Maritain concluded dourly, "there is henceforth only the earth. A complete *temporalization of Christianity!*"[66] And very often performed, strange and painful to relate, in place of—or even in the name of—the "immense renewal" of the Church that Blessed John XXIII and his ecumenical council had labored to bring about.

For progressive Catholics, the beauty of the spirit of Vatican II was precisely that it allowed them to dismiss the Council's teaching while declaring themselves the Council's champions. According to commentators like the theologian Father Richard McBrien, who taught then at Boston College and later at Notre Dame, the real achievement of Vatican II was its validation of "endless, unchecked change"

[65] Jacques Maritain, *The Peasant of the Garonne* (New York: Macmillan Paperbacks, 1969), 70–71.

[66] Ibid., 71. Emphasis in original.

as the central principle of Catholic life.[67] Yes, Pope John, in his famous speech opening the Council in 1962, had insisted that the Church should "never depart from the sacred patrimony of truth received by the fathers".[68] But once again—no matter. Father McBrien had the spirit of Vatican II. So did many others.

This line of thought's most influential representative was Giuseppe Alberigo, an Italian historian who was the principal figure in the "Bologna School" of interpreters of the Council. Alberigo, who died in 2007, was chief editor of a massive five-volume work called *History of Vatican II* (published in the United States by the left-leaning Catholic publishing house Orbis). It is an attempt to shape the interpretation of the Council for decades, even centuries, to come. A candid account of the editor's intentions can be found near the close of Alberigo's *A Brief History of Vatican II* (also from Orbis, and published in 2006).

Alberigo regards with contempt any program for the implementation of Vatican II "based upon understanding of and commentary upon the official documents".[69] The old historian insists there that what was truly important about the Council wasn't what it said and did but the process it initiated. "In the long term," he writes, "what characterizes the shift begun by the Council is the abandonment of the Counter-Reformation and the Constantinian age. This is necessarily a complex and gradual transition, and the

[67] Richard P. McBrien, *The Remaking of the Church* (New York: Harper and Row, 1973), 20.

[68] "Pope John's Opening Speech to the Council", *The Documents of Vatican II*, ed. Walter M. Abbott, S.J. (New York: America Press, 1966), 714.

[69] Giuseppe Alberigo, *A Brief History of Vatican II* (Maryknoll, N.Y.: Orbis Books, 2006), 129.

Council's contribution was to create a foundation for this and to signal its beginnings." [70]

The immediate practical consequences that thinking like that had for American Catholicism in the years after the Second Vatican Council will be seen in the next chapter, in relation to several specific areas of Church life. The present chapter is best closed with a quick look at the difficult situation created in these difficult years for that embodiment of the Americanist impulse, the Knights of Columbus, and its Supreme Knight, John W. McDevitt. To a great extent, after all, in looking at this populist Catholic organization, we are looking at American Catholicism writ large.

All but forgotten now, John McDevitt in his day was one of the most prominent and influential Catholics in America. Born in 1906 in Malden, Massachusetts, north of Boston, McDevitt received bachelor's and master's degrees from Boston College and entered upon a career as a teacher and later as principal at Malden High School. From 1942 to 1961 he was school superintendent in Waltham, Massachusetts. He also served on various school boards and was chairman of the state board of education.

A member of the Knights of Columbus for many years and at one time the organization's leader in Massachusetts, he became Deputy Supreme Knight of the K of C in 1961. Three years later he was chosen Supreme Knight. By then, the Knights had well over a million members and more than a billion dollars of insurance in force. McDevitt retired in January 1977 after a largely successful tenure devoted to guiding this grassroots fraternal society, an ideological offshoot of nineteenth-century Catholic Americanism, through

[70] Ibid., 117.

years of conflict in society and in the Church, moving it ahead cautiously on race and giving it a new "family" orientation in place of its rigidly all-male character. On matters like contraception, abortion, and the sexual revolution, as well as the Church's teaching authority, he took "a strongly conservative position", according to the Knights' official historian.[71]

McDevitt enjoyed a reputation as an orator, but his rhetoric, read now, reflects an old-fashioned ideal of orotund, somewhat windy speechifying. However, it also reflects the continuing effort of an intelligent, conservative Catholic with serious institutional responsibilities to adjust his thinking, and that of the organization he headed, to the cultural revolution that was then taking place. The central questions McDevitt sought to address in a manner meaningful to his time and place were ones we have seen often before: Is it possible to be fully Catholic and fully American? And if it is—*how*?

The evolution of McDevitt's thinking can be traced in major policy addresses delivered at the annual conventions of the K of C during the troubled late 1960s. In 1966, responding to "self-professed prophets" who pronounced the Knights of Columbus to be in "a state of helpless obsolescence", McDevitt cited new initiatives in the areas of race and ecumenism in order to refute the charge. Then he directed his attention to more fundamental matters. At the start of the K of C, he said, the organization had "served principally as a fortress where members could come together to find mutual encouragement and strength against the slings of a society still hostile to both their religion and their

---

[71] Christopher J. Kauffman, *Faith and Fraternalism: The History of the Knights of Columbus, 1882–1982* (New York: Harper and Row, 1982), 415.

nationality". Now, however, that had changed. The Catholic Church was "the leading Christian body in the land", and "it is high time we abandon the concept of our Order as mainly a fortress to protect us from a hostile world. We are not a besieged minority."[72] In the future, McDevitt insisted, the Knights should take their lead from *Gaudium et spes*, Vatican II's groundbreaking Pastoral Constitution on the Church in the Modern World, with its message of engagement with the secular order.

By 1967 his tone was significantly different. Radical left-right polarization was a visible reality in American Catholicism. So was the Knights of Columbus "a conservative or a progressive society?" McDevitt's answer: Both. The Knights were progressive in their social commitments on matters like poverty and race. But they were conservative in their Catholicism, especially in rejecting "the haughty harangue or deceiving sophism of Father So and So's latest recital on 'Why I Left the Church'". In this era of "confusion and turbulence", the group stood squarely with the hierarchy in their work of "teaching, sanctifying, and guiding the Church".[73]

Two years later, in 1969, McDevitt saw the shadows lengthening in both society and the Church. Formerly, the enemies had been outside; now they were "within the border of our country [and] within the walls of our Church". The nation's enemies he listed as "lawlessness ... injustice, poverty, discrimination ... neglect, lack of concern, and lack of dialogue". Monasteries and convents were emptying, the Supreme Knight declared, because "even among our Catholic people" many had bought into America's

---

[72] Quoted in Ibid., 405.
[73] Ibid.

"affluent, permissive, and indulgent" culture, which scorned "the spirit of discipline, self-denial and dedication". Sounding much like Leo XIII in his condemnation of Americanism, McDevitt identified the Church's internal enemies as those Catholics who acted as if everyone were "his own theologian and enjoys the infallible guidance of the Spirit" and those who broadcast "false freedom of conscience which licenses the individual to do not as God says but as the person pleases".[74]

Summing up the Knights' McDevitt years, Christopher Kauffman says that "Catholics were assimilated into the mainstream of American society, but the Knights of Columbus under John McDevitt were not fully absorbed into American culture."[75] In a world in which they and their Church were no longer comfortably at home, John McDevitt and his Knights sought a viable new expression of Catholic identity that would transcend the simplistic Americanist assumptions of their founding. Other American Catholics, similarly uneasy about the prospect of assimilation into the new cultural mainstream, also found themselves wrestling with this challenge. This too was part of the Gibbons Legacy as its implications in troubled times gradually became clearer.

[74] Ibid., 408.
[75] Ibid., 415.

3

"A FEARFUL MODERNITY"

In *Democracy in America*, reflections on the United States written after nine months spent visiting the country in 1831, Alexis de Tocqueville took a mainly sanguine view of the religion's situation. Even Catholicism, he wrote, was doing quite well under America's democratic regime; in fact, were American anti-Catholicism only to be vanquished, large numbers of Americans might actually find the Catholic Church an attractive choice for themselves. (Isaac Hecker thought the same thing, as we've seen.)

Tocqueville nevertheless concluded that the churches were not as robust as they at first appeared. Religion's acceptance in the United States, he reported, was conditioned on conformity to public opinion, which possessed supreme power under the American system. As a result:

> As men grow to be more like each other and equal to each other, it is all the more important that religions, by staying carefully away from the conduct of day-to-day affairs, avoid colliding unnecessarily with generally accepted ideas.... In America, religion is a world apart where the priest is sovereign but whose bounds he takes care never to leave. Within its limits, he guides intelligence; outside, he leaves men to their own devices.... Although American Christians are divided into a mass of sects, they all view their religion in

this same light, which applies to Catholicism as much as to other beliefs.[1]

Here's one more example of the perceptiveness of a very perceptive man.

In many ways, the 1960s now seem as remote in time from both the 1830s and the American Catholic present as, say, Jupiter is remote in space from planet Earth. But the real continuity that exists is important to our story.

Writing on the cusp of the sixties, the Jewish sociologist of religion Will Herberg took note of the fact that by the time of the post–World War II religious boom, the United States was religiously tripartite: Protestant-Catholic-Jew.[2] Many Americans probably received this news as welcome affirmation from the discipline of sociology of something in which they already took no little pride—the toleration and mutual acceptance alongside religious pluralism that by now was an established part of the American Way.

Yet Herberg did not mean that all was entirely well on the American religious scene. Comity had a price, which he described in a paper delivered in 1959 at the University of Notre Dame. The "three great faiths", in their eagerness to be American, had sacrificed a significant measure of their own special identities.

"Just as Americans are coming more and more to think of being a Protestant, being a Catholic, and being a Jew as three alternative ways of being an American, so they are coming to regard Protestantism, Catholicism, and Judaism . . . as three alternative (though not necessarily equal) expressions of a

---

[1] Alexis de Tocqueville, *Democracy in America*, trans. Gerald E. Bevan (London: Penguin Books, 2003), 517.

[2] See Will Herberg, *Protestant, Catholic, Jew* (New York: Doubleday, 1955), passim.

great overarching commitment which they all share by virtue of being Americans. This commitment is, of course, democracy or the American Way of Life." [3]

Driving the point home, Herberg quoted a remark attributed to President Eisenhower shortly after his election in 1952: "Our government makes no sense unless it is founded in a deeply felt religious faith, and I don't care what it is." Herberg commented:

> And why didn't he care which it was? Because, in his view, as in the view of all normal Americans, they "all say the same thing." And what is the "same thing" which they all say? The answer is given to us from the current vocabulary: "the moral and spiritual values of democracy." These, for the typical American, are in a real sense final and ultimate; the three conventional religions are approved of and validated primarily because they embody and express these "moral and spiritual values of democracy." [4]

Shades of Tocqueville!

Lest anyone miss his point, Herberg went on to explain that what he was describing was "essentially the 'Americanization' of religion in America, and therefore also its thoroughgoing secularization". American Protestantism had been experiencing this since after the Civil War; now, in the middle years of the twentieth century, it had spread to Catholicism and Judaism: "With the loss of their foreignness, of their immigrant marginality, these two religious groups seem to be losing their capacity to resist dissolution in the culture." [5]

---

[3] Will Herberg, "Religion and Culture in Present-Day America", in *Roman Catholicism and the American Way of Life*, ed. Thomas T. McAvoy, C.S.C. (Notre Dame, Ind.: University of Notre Dame Press, 1960), 11.

[4] Ibid., 12.

[5] Ibid., 13–14.

Herberg spoke before the tumultuous 1960s began. It seems likely that he would have found much in that decade to show how, as might have been expected, culturally assimilated Protestantism, Catholicism, and Judaism were swept up in the cultural revolution of the times.

The collection of essays in which Herberg's analysis appeared also contained a paper by Joseph H. Fichter, S.J., a prominent Catholic sociologist, observing that American Catholic values and practices were already in "a state of ambivalence". He explained: "The laws of the Church concerning mixed marriage, birth prevention, attendance at Catholic schools, and others, tend to meet head-on the ways of thinking and acting that have developed in our urban, secular, industrial society." [6]

Before the decade was out, another sociologist of religion, Peter Berger, took a fresh look at the Catholic Church and saw something new at work there: the Second Vatican Council. Long before then, he wrote, there'd been "undercurrents of accommodation and modernization" in Catholicism, but "the pumps ... began to gush with Vatican II", and in "Catholic intellectual milieux, the very milieux in which the theological enterprise must be socially rooted, there have of late emerged noises of a fearful modernity sufficient to put the most 'radical' Protestant to shame". [7]

Berger was correct in identifying "intellectual milieux" as the locus of origin for this process in Catholicism, but the *pastoral* consequences of the sudden eruption into popular Catholicism of accommodation and modernization were

---

[6] Joseph H. Fichter, S.J., "The Americanization of Catholicism", in McAvoy, *Roman Catholicism*, 123.

[7] Peter L. Berger, *A Rumor of Angels: Modern Society and the Rediscovery of the Supernatural* (Garden City, N.Y.: Anchor Books, 1970), 13.

in some respects even more marked than the academic, intellectual ones. These consequences were quickly to become visible in defections from the priesthood and religious life, a precipitous drop in new priestly and religious vocations; confusion among lay Catholics regarding the practical meaning of being a Catholic; and the spiritual and physical withdrawal of many Catholics from the sacramental life of the Church as measured by things like Sunday Mass attendance, reception of the sacrament of penance ("going to confession"), and marrying in the Church. Unknown to most people then, in retrospect the consequences can now also be seen in the sudden rise in the sexual abuse of children by Catholic priests that took place at this time.[8]

As the 1960s rolled on, something that resembled hysteria seemed to grip many of the faithful. Often with encouragement from above,[9] they cited the activity of the Holy Spirit to explain and rationalize their strange behavior. Pope Leo XIII had foreseen this seven decades earlier in *Testem benevolentiae* when he spoke of Catholics who rejected the teaching office of the Church as "superfluous, nay even as useless" on the grounds that "the Holy Spirit now pours

[8] See *The Causes and Context of Sexual Abuse of Minors by Catholic Priests in the United States, 1950–2010: A Report Presented to the United States Conference of Catholic Bishops by the John Jay College Research Team* (Washington, D.C.: United States Conference of Catholic Bishops, 2011), 26–34.

[9] As in this: "One will have to proceed with courage—sometimes the real name for prudence—and with imagination, but above all with a lively faith in the Holy Spirit 'who blows where he will,' and who seems at this moment to be opening up new paths and entering ever more deeply into the life of the Church.... [I]t is reassuring to keep in mind that the Holy Spirit is indefectibly present in his Church through the weaknesses and gropings of men, and that he animates it from within so that the Church might find that fresh renewing breeze of the Spirit, which is none other than the initial wind, that of Pentecost." Leo-Jozef Suenens, preface to *The Remaking of the Church*, by Richard P. McBrien (New York: Harper and Row, 1973), x.

forth into the souls of the faithful more and richer gifts than in times past, and, with no intermediary, by a kind of hidden instinct teaches and moves them." [10]

Along with the Holy Spirit, another spirit—"the spirit of Vatican II"—was now regularly invoked by ecclesiastical innovators in a rhetorical maneuver that sought to enlist the Council on their side, either with—or, more often, without—support from the documents that Vatican II had debated, amended, and adopted. We shall see more about this below. Here it's enough to say that this double-teaming in the name of the two "spirits" delivered a powerful pneumatic assault on the settled order of Catholic life.

Walker Percy pointed to the results in *Love in the Ruins*, a futuristic novel published in 1971 about the decline and fall of just about everything and everybody. Percy saw emerging an American Catholicism that would be "split into three pieces"—the American Catholic Church, headquartered in Cicero, Illinois, emphasizing property rights and celebrating Mass in Latin, with "The Star-Spangled Banner" sung at the elevation of the Host; the Dutch schismatics, mostly former priests and nuns, some married and some now divorced and seeking permission to remarry, who "believe in relevance but not God"; and the Roman Catholic remnant, "a tiny scattered flock with no place to go".[11] Readers found this funny but also slightly grim.

It's well beyond the scope of the present book to take a comprehensive look at American Catholicism since 1960. A few snapshots must suffice. The themes to be examined here briefly are the rise of the culture of dissent, Catholic

[10] *Testem benevolentiae*, January 22, 1899, in Henry Denziger, *The Sources of Catholic Dogma*, trans. Roy J. Deferrari (St. Louis: B. Herder, 1957), 499.

[11] Walker Percy, *Love in the Ruins* (New York: Avon Books, 1978), 5–6.

participation in politics and public life, Catholic higher education, confusion and conflict within the hierarchy, and clergy sex abuse.

1. The Culture of Dissent

Humanae Vitae, the encyclical in which Pope Paul VI reaffirmed the Church's teaching against contraception, was published in late July of 1968. An angry howl of dissent quickly arose from numerous theologians in North America and western Europe. The Sunday after the encyclical was published, with this opposition by now much in the news, I went to Mass as usual at Holy Trinity Church, a trendy Jesuit parish in the Georgetown section of the nation's capital where John and Jacqueline Kennedy had worshiped before moving to the White House. When it was time for the homily, the priest climbed into the pulpit and launched his explanation of why Catholics were right to dissent from *Humanae vitae*. When he finished, most members of the congregation applauded. I did not. That sermon, and the applause that greeted it, were my own introduction to the full-blown culture of dissent—and also to the postconciliar era in full bloom.

The Second Vatican Council (1962–1965) had called for the renewal of the Church, but by the summer of 1968 something very different had set in. Approvingly citing President Lyndon Johnson's announcement that he wouldn't seek reelection because of public unhappiness with the undeclared war in Vietnam, the Jesuit weekly *America*, in its issue of August 17, recommended that Pope Paul VI follow LBJ's example and resign. Honest efforts at Church renewal were henceforth to continue here and there, but it was clear that an organized culture of dissent now existed as a highly visible presence in American Catholicism and had become the

medium through which the renewal of the Church henceforth would be interpreted to not a few American Catholics, including many clergy and religious.

Back in 1950, *The Cardinal* had depicted Stephen Fermoyle's resistance to arrogant Planned Parenthood activists
as a brave—and popular—act. Nevertheless, the Catholic
Church's position on birth control by then had been widely
criticized outside the Church for years, and priests in
the trenches were all too well aware that many of their
parishioners were contracepting.[12] By the early 1960s, cracks
also had begun to appear in the consensus of Catholic
moral theologians. Finally, in 1967, more than a year
before *Humanae vitae*, the stage for large-scale public dissent was set at the U.S. bishops' own institution of higher
learning, the Catholic University of America in Washington, D.C.

Father Charles Curran, a young teacher of moral theology already well known for his rejection of Church teaching on birth control and other issues, sought promotion to
the rank of associate professor. His department and the faculty senate approved, but the university's board of trustees
vetoed the action and voted 28–1 not to renew the priest's
contract. A strike by angry faculty and students, resembling the protests that had occurred, or soon would occur,
on many other campuses in that era when protest was in
vogue, then shut down Catholic University. The trustees
retreated, the priest got what he wanted, and life went
on—after a fashion. In 1968, using the Catholic University as his base of operations, Father Curran spearheaded
American dissent from *Humanae vitae* by theologians and
others allied with them. Not until 1986, after the Vatican's

---

[12] See, for example, Fichter, "Americanization", 123.

Congregation for the Doctrine of the Faith, headed by Joseph Cardinal Ratzinger, declared that Curran's views made him ineligible to teach Catholic theology, was the priest finally forced out of Catholic University. He then went to court but lost.

Dissent rapidly spread to other issues besides contraception: masturbation, contraceptive sterilization, divorce, artificial insemination, in vitro fertilization, homosexual acts, abortion, and euthanasia. Nor was dissent limited to moral questions. In due course, it came also to extend to Christology, soteriology, and other areas of theology, increasingly taking on the character of a culture, as an infrastructure of sympathetic organizations, schools, periodicals, and publishing houses took shape and lent it support.

While these developments were still in their early stages, the American bishops in November 1968 made a serious tactical error in their collective pastoral letter presenting their response to *Humanae vitae* along with their views on the Vietnam War.[13] Although the document expressed support for the pope's condemnation of artificial birth control, it took a notably tolerant view of what it styled "licit dissent". As Kenneth Whitehead points out, however, the bishops' tolerance assumes a model of dissent as an "academic-style doubt or disagreement ... within the groves of academe". In reality, as was already perfectly clear by then, dissent had become "open revolt against the teaching authority of the Church, consciously designed to persuade the faithful".[14] In effect, the bishops in 1968 were giving

---

[13] "Human Life in Our Day", November 15, 1968, www.ewtn.com/library/bishops/USBPSHV.htm.

[14] Kenneth D. Whitehead, *The Renewed Church: The Second Vatican Council's Enduring Teaching about the Church* (Ave Maria, Fla.: Sapientia Press, 2009), 88–89.

dissenting theologians a license to dissent. Many have continued to do that ever since, despite occasional appeals to the dissenters to stop—that have emanated from the pope, the Congregation for the Doctrine of the Faith, the doctrine committee of the bishops' conference, and individual bishops.

Blunders in implementing the Council did not help the situation. At the American bishops' post–Vatican II meeting held in Washington, D.C., in November 1966, the bishops, acting with little or no advance public notice, abolished the rule requiring Catholics to abstain from meat on Fridays. A small thing in itself, fish on Friday nevertheless had been a highly visible feature of Catholic religious identity for generations, helping to set Catholics apart from others and making a statement to the world: "We're Catholics, and we aren't like everyone else." Now abruptly abolishing Friday abstinence sent a very different message: Things the Church previously had emphasized could be discarded like a pair of worn-out shoes. This mistake would be repeated many times in the postconciliar years, especially in the area of liturgy.

As time went by, however, it soon became clear that the underlying issue was Vatican II itself. Or, more precisely, how the Council ought to be understood. We saw above how dissenters learned to set "the spirit of Vatican II" against the actual teaching of Vatican II, as a tactic for pressing their case for an open-ended process of radical change in the Church. Forty years later, in a Christmas 2005 address to the Roman Curia, Pope Benedict XVI famously framed the interpretation of Vatican II in terms of two opposed hermeneutics—a "hermeneutic of discontinuity and rupture" and a "hermeneutic of reform" embracing "renewal in the continuity of the one subject-Church". He made it clear he supported the latter.[15]

But by no means has that been the end of the argument. Consider a recent book-length apologetic for the hermeneutic of discontinuity that can fairly be taken as a representative example of this school of thought.

In *The American Catholic Revolution*, Father Mark Massa, S.J., dean of the school of theology and ministry at Boston College, cites with approval Bernard Lonergan's claim that the "real issue" behind intra-Church arguments in the 1960s and 1970s was "the transition from a classicist worldview to historical-mindedness". From this perspective, Father Massa says, conservatives are wasting their time stressing the continuity between Vatican II and its predecessors.

> No matter what the (essentially conservative) intentions of the person who originally called that council (Good Pope John XXIII), or of the overwhelming majority of Catholic bishops who approved the reforms of the council, ... the unsettling new historical consciousness unleashed by the council's reforms could not be stopped by anything so simple as an appeal to the intentions of the council's participants, or to some purported "law of continuity" within the tradition.[16]

Father Massa declares Lonergan's "transition from a classicist worldview to historical-mindedness" an accurate formulation for expressing "the intellectual revolution that

---

[15] "Address to the Members of the Roman Curia", December 22, 2005, www.vatican.va/holy_father/Benedict_xvi/speeches/2005/december/documents/hf_ben_xvi_spe_20051222_roman-curia_en.html.

[16] Mark S. Massa, S.J., *The American Catholic Revolution: How the '60s Changed the Church Forever* (New York: Oxford University Press, 2010), 13.

mainstream Catholics underwent during the sixties".[17] Other Catholics, tempted perhaps to take this as some sort of parody, need to recognize that the author of these words actually shares the point of view they describe. There are two things to be said about that.

First, calling the experience of ordinary American Catholics in the 1960s a transition from a classicist world view to historical mindedness strains credulity to its breaking point. To be sure, ordinary Catholics in large numbers were bowled over by the cultural revolution of those years—in particular, the sexual revolution—and they and the Church are still reeling from the effects of that. But this was merely an instance of succumbing to an aberrant zeitgeist. Some academic intellectuals may choose to call it a transition from one world view to another, but the "mainstream" knows better.

Second, people who think like this are correct in situating Vatican II at a particular point in a historical process that, faith tells us, will continue to the end of time. But Catholics for centuries have taken it for granted that the doctrinal pronouncements and disciplinary decisions of ecumenical councils acting in union with the pope have real normative force: the teaching must be assented to, the legislation obeyed, by those who wish to be within the communion of the Church. In the end, continuity is important because of the presence and action of the Holy Spirit in this teaching, legislating community of faith. Father Massa quotes John Henry Newman's aphorism, "To live is to change; and to live long is to have changed often", but he neglects to point out that Newman said this in the first chapter of his *Essay on the Development of Christian Doctrine*, whose central point is not change but the profound continuity of the

[17] Ibid., 160.

Catholic tradition.[18] By contrast, the ruinous thrust of the Lonergan argument is that no proposition about God formulated in a way we can understand can be more than an unsatisfactory attempt to express the inexpressible.

Finally, then, where do American dissenters wish to take the Church? No one Magna Carta sets out the consensus of this body of opinion. A friend of mine suggests that the long-range goal of progressive Catholics can be summed up as "Archbishop Patricia of Chicago attending a pro-choice rally with her partner Susan", but, leaving that aside, let us take as typical the words of a somewhat prominent member of the group. I turn to a paper presented by Dr. Paul Lakeland on September 17, 2010, to a "Synod of the Baptized" convened in Minneapolis–Saint Paul by a group calling itself the Catholic Coalition for Church Reform.[19] Dr. Lakeland, a former Jesuit from Lancashire, England, has written several books and is a professor of Catholic studies at the Jesuits' Fairfield University in Connecticut, where he has taught since 1981.

The paper contains much to recommend it, including its extended treatment of the sacrament of baptism and its vocational implications for the laity. Even when it comes to practical proposals, Lakeland is, for the most part, fairly bland. He names "three developments that would materially affect our community of faith for the better". These are "a two-way structure of communication and accountability", "good liturgy", and insisting that the Church's

---

[18] Father Massa also gets the quotation wrong. Newman wrote that "to live is to change, and to be perfect is to have changed often." John Henry Newman, *Essay on the Development of Christian Doctrine* (Garden City, N.Y.: Image Books, 1960), 62.

[19] The paper, entitled "The Call of the Baptized: Be the Church, Live the Mission", is available on the coalition's website: www.cccrmn.org (click on "Recommended Reading" and then "Ecclesiology").

"ordained ministers attend to the spiritual welfare of the people and ... leave the mission of the Church to the world in the hands of us, the experts" (the laity, that is). Taken at face value, there is little to object to in these generalities, although it is a crucial—and here unanswered—question how Lakeland would flesh them out in practical policies and programs if he had the opportunity.

There is, however, a hint about that at the paper's very end, and it is unnerving. "The Church", Dr. Lakeland declares, "is a school of love. The role of the institution vis-à-vis baptized Catholics is to let them loose to love, not to bind them with rules about who or how to love. The future health of the Church depends upon recovering that sense of itself."

Ah, love. Who can argue with it? This is part of the conventional discourse, apparently meant for popular consumption, of the culture of dissent. But love without specified content? Love that in principle excludes no mode of expressing it? Love divorced from "rules"—which is to say, from principles and norms? The Old and New Testaments and the Christian tradition contain many rules commanding and forbidding specific behavior. Not all these rules, especially some dating to Old Testament times, are relevant today, but many are. Does the understanding of love embraced by people like Lakeland extend to a gay man's sexual expression of love for his same-sex partner, the love of a doctor who aborts an unborn child with Down Syndrome lest the child be a burden to the parents, adulterous love like Anna Karenina's for Vronsky in Tolstoy's novel, the love of an Islamic fundamentalist who blows himself up in a marketplace to demonstrate his love for Allah, the love of a nurse who overdoses an old woman far gone in Alzheimer's with a sedative from which she'll never awaken? Love without rules often takes troubling forms.

Admittedly, though, rules do get in the way of realizing that "historical consciousness" celebrated by Father Massa and others who think as he does. The idea of historical consciousness appears to have entered the Catholic bloodstream via Modernists like Alfred Loisy and George Tyrrell. Lakeland's words about the Church as a school of love with no rules on "who or how" to love, recall something Tyrrell said in his book *Medievalism*, which was published shortly before his death in 1909; the passage stands as a good account of the beliefs that undergird today's neo-Modernism. Praising "life and movement" as opposed to "stagnation and death", Tyrrell wrote: "To believe in the living historical Catholic community means to believe that by its corporate life and labour it is slowly realizing the ideas and ends in whose service it was founded.... One's belief in the Church as the organ of religion is to some extent one's belief in the laws of collective psychology, which are the laws of nature, which are the laws of God."[20]

Poor George Tyrrell. Expelled from the Society of Jesus and excommunicated from the Church, perhaps he was unaware that the trajectory of his optimistic evolutionism implied a Christianity of his imagining that would improve on the Christianity that Christianity's founder had chosen to provide.

2. Politics: Houston and Beyond

In 1935 the Massachusetts state legislature was weighing a measure to establish a state lottery. William Cardinal O'Connell of Boston thought doing that would be a bad

---

[20] Quoted in Marvin R. O'Connell, *Critics on Trial: An Introduction to the Catholic Modernist Crisis* (Washington, D.C.: Catholic University of America Press, 1994), 373.

idea. The cardinal shared his views with the newspapers, and reports of his remarks "caused half the legislature to change its mind, sending the bill down to lopsided defeat by sunset". Similar weight, we are told, was given to O'Connell's positions on other issues, including birth control. Around the Massachusetts State House, people referred to him simply as "Number One".[21] Everybody knew who that meant.

But times do change.

In 2009 Patrick Kennedy, son of the late senator Edward Kennedy of Massachusetts and at the time himself a member of the U.S. House of Representatives from Rhode Island, became locked in an ugly dispute with his ordinary, Bishop Thomas Tobin of Providence. The issue was legalized abortion and the American bishops' opposition to funding for abortion in the health care bill that was then before Congress.

Kennedy, a Catholic with a pro-choice position on abortion, accused the hierarchy of creating "discord and dissent" by opposing the inclusion of abortion in the health bill. At the height of the quarrel, he claimed Bishop Tobin had "instructed" him not to receive Communion and had told diocesan priests not to give it to him. The bishop then released a letter from two years earlier in which he wrote the congressman, "I . . . ask respectfully that you refrain [from receiving Communion]"; there was no indication that he'd said anything to diocesan priests. Publicly, neither man backed down. Kennedy later decided not to seek reelection.

The Massachusetts legislature's obsequious attitude toward Cardinal O'Connell back in 1935 was no healthier than

Patrick Kennedy's defiance of Bishop Tobin in 2009. But that isn't the point. The question here is how to account for the dramatic shift from obsequiousness to defiance that had taken place in those 74 years. A fully satisfying answer would take many pages and be beyond the scope of this book. But it's fair to say that a landmark event paving the way for a great deal else occurred in Houston, Texas, on September 12, 1960, when John F. Kennedy, U.S. senator from Massachusetts and Democratic candidate for president of the United States, spoke to the Greater Houston Ministerial Association.

Kennedy had grown up in the Massachusetts church-state environment in which easy domination of the state legislature by the archbishop of Boston was taken for granted. The early phases of his political career found him raising no objection. By 1960, however, Kennedy knew that, except for Massachusetts and a few other places, his membership in the Catholic Church and the Church's role in politics were serious obstacles to his election as president.[22] How serious became alarmingly clear in September, at the height of the presidential campaign, when Dr. Norman Vincent Peale, a popular preacher and author of a best seller called *The Power of Positive Thinking*, headed a group of 150 prominent Protestants who maintained on religious grounds that no practicing Catholic could be fit to hold America's highest elective office. The Catholic Church, according to a

---

[22] The role of the religious issue in the Kennedy campaign of 1960 is discussed in a number of places, including John T. McGreevy, *Catholicism and American Freedom* (New York: Norton, 2003); William B. Prendergast, *The Catholic Voter in American Politics: The Passing of the Democratic Monolith* (Washington, D.C.: Georgetown University Press, 1999); and George J. Marlin, *The American Catholic Voter: 200 Years of Political Impact* (South Bend, Ind.: St. Augustine's Press, 2004).

joint statement by Peale and his associates, was a "political as well as a religious organization" that sought to break down the wall of separation between church and state. And a Catholic like Kennedy, if elected president, would be unable to "withstand the determined efforts of the hierarchy to work its will in American political life".[23]

This was hardly the first time that suspicion regarding the political intentions and loyalties of Catholics entered into American politics. Nativist bigotry had flared up periodically during the nineteenth century, and as recently as 1928, as we've seen, hostility to Catholics and their Church had been a major factor in the defeat of Al Smith, the Catholic governor of New York and that year's Democratic candidate for president.

The deep-seated resentments which that outcome fed among Catholics were in time to redound to Kennedy's advantage. I still remember the Dominican nun who one day—this must have been around 1945 or 1946—interrupted the routine of math drill in order to speak to my parochial school class in hushed tones of righteous anger about the foul injustice visited on Catholics by the ugly events of 1928. Little did she or any of us know then that she was indoctrinating Kennedy voters of 1960.

John Kennedy, Harvard graduate, war hero, scion of a wealthy and politically ambitious Boston Catholic family, had begun his remote preparation for a run at the White House in 1946 with a successful campaign for the House of Representatives. Ten years later he decided to seek his party's vice-presidential nomination, battling it out with Senator Estes Kefauver of Tennessee at the Democratic convention in Chicago. Kefauver won, and the Adlai Stevenson–Kefauver

---

[23] Quoted in Prendergast, *Catholic Voter in American Politics*, 139.

ticket was overwhelmed in November by the GOP's Dwight Eisenhower and Richard Nixon. But Kennedy's able performance at the convention and during the campaign guaranteed that he would be taken seriously four years later.

And he was. After slugging it out in the Democratic primaries with Senator Hubert H. Humphrey of Minnesota, Kennedy was nominated for president at the party's national convention in Los Angeles in July. Hoping to tamp down the anti-Catholicism that had already surfaced here and there and win the South, he tapped Senate majority leader Lyndon Johnson, a Texan, as his running mate.

But the anti-Catholicism persisted, reaching a peak in September with the statement by the Peale group. Richard Nixon, Kennedy's Republican opponent, had spurned exploitation of the religious issue and now publicly defended Kennedy's patriotism. But the harm was done. The Peale document touched off a firestorm of media coverage and commentary, provided new legitimacy for old anti-Catholic fears, and brought bigots out of the woodwork in droves.

Now Kennedy made a crucial decision: he would confront the Catholic issue head-on in a major speech. The result, his September 12 address to the ministers in Houston, is one of the most significant American political utterances of the twentieth century.

Part of it is simple pandering of the sort that politicians seeking office routinely indulge in. As a young congressman representing the Boston district that was earlier represented by his own grandfather, John "Honey Fitz" Fitzgerald, and legendary Boston mayor James Michael Curley (the model for the central character in Edwin O'Connor's classic novel of Boston Irish politics, *The Last Hurrah*), Kennedy was a reliable supporter of the Church's positions on political issues. But now, to the Houston ministers, he proudly cited his "declared stands against an ambassador to the Vatican, against unconstitutional aid to parochial schools, and against any boycott of the public schools". He also declared his support for "absolute" separation of church and state.[24]

The conceptual heart of the Houston speech is, however, its powerful thrust in the direction of privatizing religion in line with American secularist thinking. The speech operates on two levels: the level of politics and public life, and the private, personal level of individual conscience. In both realms, the message is an implicit but devastating assault on traditional Catholic ways of thinking about these matters.

On the public-political level, the Kennedy text employs the familiar rhetorical device of setting up false options in order to reject them. "I believe", the candidate affirmed, "in an America that is officially neither Catholic, Protestant nor Jewish—where no public official either requests or accepts instructions on public policy from the pope, the National Council of Churches or any other ecclesiastical source."[25] It would of course have been hard to say what public official in 1960 *did* seek or conceivably *would have* sought instructions from these sources.

More radical was his declaration of belief in an America "where no religious body seeks to impose its will directly or indirectly upon the general populace or the public acts of its officials".[26] Did this exclude religious bodies from joining the public debate and trying to persuade others of

[24] Address of Senator John F. Kennedy to the Greater Houston Ministerial Association, September 12, 1960, John F. Kennedy Presidential Library and Museum, http://www.jfklibrary.org/JFK/Historic-Speeches/Multilingual-Address-to-the-Greater-Houston-Ministerial-Association.aspx.

[25] Ibid.

[26] Ibid.

the rightness of their positions? Apparently so. The unspoken assumption underlying the speech is that in America religion should have nothing to say to politics: docile, domesticated churches should keep their noses out of the substance of public life. Tocqueville had predicted this 130 years earlier.

On the question of conscience, the candidate made this pledge: "Whatever issue may come before me as president—on birth control, divorce, censorship, gambling or any other subject—I will make my decision ... in accordance with what my conscience tells me to be in the national interest, and without regard to outside religious pressures or dictates." [27] In this way the criterion of policy is identified not just as the national interest, but national interest as defined by the private judgment of the president without reference to moral principles from religious sources ("pressures" and "dictates"). Are other sources besides religious sources also excluded? Kennedy didn't say. Then what sources might be permitted to have a role in shaping a president's conscience? The Houston speech also is silent on this. Altogether an odd performance, one might be pardoned for thinking.

Father John Courtney Murray, S.J., the preeminent American Catholic theologian on matters of church and state at the time, was consulted by Kennedy's people in formulating the candidate's position. Whatever Father Murray may have told them, it's hard to believe he was altogether pleased with the Houston text. Several years later, writing of Vatican II's Declaration on Religious Freedom, *Dignitatis humanae*, which he helped to write, Murray called the idea that "I have a right to do what my conscience tells me to do, simply because my conscience tells me to do it" a "perilous

[27] Ibid.

theory" that ended in "subjectivism" and was not at all what the Council taught.[28]

Another Catholic consulted by the Kennedy people was John Cogley, a former executive editor of *Commonweal* and a columnist for that lay-edited journal. Cogley was later to become the religion writer for the *New York Times* and would cover the close of Vatican II for that newspaper. Eventually he quit the Catholic Church and became an Episcopalian; he was an Episcopal deacon when he died. In a November 2004 editorial marking the 80th anniversary of JFK's address, *Commonweal* said this about events surrounding the speech:

> One of the key figures coaching Kennedy for his Houston appearance was John Cogley.... Kennedy had written an article in *Look* magazine in 1959 [actually, it was an interview with journalist Fletcher Knebel] in which he enunciated the view that for an "officeholder no moral obligation transcends the duty to live up to the Constitution." ... In his *Commonweal* column, Cogley defended Kennedy, insisting that an "officeholder's" first duty was indeed to the Constitution. If a conflict arose between Catholic morality and the Constitution, a Catholic officeholder should resign, Cogley wrote [a position Kennedy later famously made his own].
>
> Kennedy read Cogley's column, and asked him to join his campaign staff. ... Traveling with the future president to Houston, Cogley was charged with putting him through some "instant theological training." Cogley thought that one remark Kennedy made during their time together was especially revealing: "It is hard for a Harvard man to answer questions in theology. My answers tonight will probably cause heartburn at Fordham and BC [Boston College]."

[28] Murray makes this observation in footnote 5 of his important commentary on the Vatican II document: Walter M. Abbott, S.J., ed., *The Documents of Vatican II* (New York: Guild Press, 1966), 679.

Whether there was or wasn't heartburn on the campuses of those two Jesuit schools, Kennedy's remarks helped greatly in getting him elected president. And Cogley? "History suggests", *Commonweal* commented, that although Cogley was right about many things, nevertheless in this instance he "mistook the veneer of Kennedy's Catholicism for depth, and similarly underestimated the challenge a powerful secularizing culture would present to the coherence and vitality of a church no longer rooted in a separate Catholic subculture".[29]

John Kennedy's Houston speech was delivered more than a dozen years before the Supreme Court's January 22, 1973, decision in *Roe v. Wade* that legalized abortion throughout the United States and radically altered the moral and political landscape of the nation, of the Catholic Church, and of Catholics within the Democratic Party. For many such Catholics, however, and in due course many other Catholics as well, theological groundwork for accepting the doctrine of *Roe* had been laid in 1964 at Robert Kennedy's home in the Kennedy compound at Hyannisport, Massachusetts. Organized by brother-in-law Sargent Shriver, the meeting featured the participation of Father Robert Drinan, S.J., dean of the Boston College law school and later a member of Congress; Dr. Andre E. Hellegers, founder and first director of the Kennedy Institute of Ethics at Georgetown University; and five Catholic moral theologians: Fathers Joseph Fuchs, S.J., Richard McCormick, S.J., Giles Millhaven, S.J., Albert Jonsen, S.J., and Charles Curran.

The meeting was convened to help Bobby Kennedy and his younger brother Ted find a position, acceptable to the Catholic Church, that would hold to the immorality of

---

[29] "A Catholic President?", *Commonweal*, November 5, 2004.

abortion "but not argue for its legal prohibition".[30] Even so, Ted Kennedy remained publicly pro-life at least until 1971, when he wrote to a constituent: "When history looks back to this era it should recognize this generation as one which cared about human beings enough to halt the practice of war, to provide a decent living for every family, and to fulfill its responsibility to children from the moment of conception." After *Roe v. Wade*, Kennedy turned pro-choice, becoming an iconic figure of the abortion movement.

He was hardly alone. Over the years, the roll call of Catholic politicians who support abortion has grown longer and longer. They include Geraldine Ferraro, Democratic presidential candidate Walter Mondale's running mate in 1984, who brought the wrath of New York cardinal John O'Connor down on her head by asserting that a Catholic like herself was entitled to be pro-choice; New York governor Mario Cuomo, often mentioned as a potential presidential candidate himself, who made the case for the "personally opposed to abortion" line in a famous 1984 speech at the University of Notre Dame; Senator John Kerry (D-MA), the 2004 Democratic presidential contender, whose recollections of having been an altar boy couldn't conceal his deep ignorance of the Catholic Church; and, at the present time, former Speaker of the House Nancy Pelosi, Vice President Joseph Biden, and a host of other Catholic senators, representatives, and holders of public office at the national, state, and local levels who claim to see no conflict between their religious profession and their support for legalized abortion. To one degree or another, all of these pro-choice Catholics can trace the

[30] J. Brian Benestad, "Robert Drinan, S.J. and Catholic Moral Theologians Failed the Kennedys on Abortion in 1964", *FCS Quarterly* 34 (Spring 2011): 78–79. Many accounts of this meeting have been published, including by participants Jonsen and Millhaven.

intellectual roots of their position on abortion to JFK's words in Houston in September 1960. Many are actively involved in the campaign by secularists in and out of government to coerce church-sponsored enterprises like schools, hospitals, and Catholic Charities to adopt secularist values in relation to issues like contraception, abortion, and same-sex marriage or else go out of business.[31]

And so? As a new Congress was getting under way early in 2011, political columnist Michael Gerson, a conservative with a sensitivity to issues of social justice, called attention to the fact that the number of Catholic Republicans in the House of Representatives had risen to 64 and nearly equaled the Democratic Catholics' total of 68. What difference would this make? "Judging from the broader behavior of Catholics in American politics," Gerson wrote, "not much."

He explained: "A century ago, many Catholics voted Democratic out of ethnic solidarity. Today, most Catholics vote almost exactly like their suburban neighbors. Catholics are often swing voters in elections precisely because they are so typical." Gerson didn't regard this as good news. "There is something vaguely disturbing", he observed, "about the precise symmetry of any religious group with other voters of their same class and background. One would hope that an ancient, demanding faith would leave some distinctive mark."[32]

The Catholic tradition has within it the capacity to leave such a mark, but imprinting it upon American politics here and now requires the active cooperation of Catholics in public life. As to the tradition, five years after John Kennedy's

[31] Russell Shaw, "New Tensions between Bishops, White House", *Our Sunday Visitor*, October 23, 2011; "An Uphill Slog for the Bishops", *National Catholic Reporter*, October 14, 2011.

[32] Michael Gerson, "A Catholic Test for Politics", *Washington Post*, February 8, 2011.

Houston speech, on December 6, 1965, the fathers of the
Second Vatican Council completed their work by adopting
the Pastoral Constitution on the Church in the Modern
World, *Gaudium et spes*, by a vote of 2,111–251. Among
other things, the pastoral constitution skewers the state of
mind that Kennedy's remarks not only reflected but helped
give legitimacy.

While conceding that "we have here no lasting city",
the Council nevertheless said:

> "It is no less mistaken to think that we may immerse our-
> selves in earthly activities as if these latter were utterly for-
> eign to religion, and religion were nothing more than the
> fulfillment of acts of worship and the observance of a few
> moral obligations. One of the gravest errors of our time is
> the dichotomy between the faith which many profess and
> the practice of their daily lives." [33]

Houston notwithstanding, so it was then, and so it remains
now.

3. The Worst Year Ever

There are basically two opposed versions of the story of American Catholicism in the years since Vatican II. Which of these
a person subscribes to is usually a good indicator of where
he stands on many crucial issues in the life of the Church.

The first version divides the postconciliar era into two
parts. The first, starting with the Council's close in 1965
and continuing until late 1978, was marked by turmoil and

[33] Vatican Council II, Pastoral Constitution on the Church in the Mod-
ern World, *Gaudium et spes*, no. 43, in *Vatican Council II: The Conciliar and
Post Conciliar Documents*, edited by Austin Flannery, O.P. (Northport, N.Y.:
Costello). All quotations from the Vatican II documents are from this edition.

dissent mirroring the cultural revolution that was then taking place in society. Thousands of priests and religious quit the priesthood and religious life, while new priestly and religious vocations fell precipitously. After the brave gesture of *Humanae vitae* in 1968—and the violent reaction against it—Pope Paul VI grew increasingly weary and depressed. The "smoke of Satan" had entered the Church, he declared, and it was smothering the Vatican II renewal. Indeed, at times the Church appeared to be rushing toward collapse. But 1978 brought the election of Pope John Paul II, and collapse was averted.

The second version of the story divides the same stretch of time in the same way, but it interprets the two segments very differently. In this view, the years from 1965 to 1978 take on the aura of a golden age for the Church in America. Heroic progressives battled reactionaries over the direction of Church renewal and, except for a few setbacks like *Humanae vitae*, generally emerged victorious. But then came 1978, the death of Paul VI, and the election, following the month-long pontificate of John Paul I (the "smiling pope", who apparently died of anxiety and stress), of John Paul II. Suddenly Rome's emphasis became thwarting renewal and turning back the clock. This project of restoration is believed to have continued under Benedict XVI.

Against this background, what was the worst year ever for the Catholic Church in the United States? For many people, the obvious answer is 2002. That was when disclosures of sexual abuse of children by priests and its cover-up by Church authorities came spilling out—first in Boston, then in dioceses across the country—causing scandal and outrage at what had transpired. Indeed, 2002 was a very bad year (but what happened then, agonizing though it was, had to occur for the purification of the Church).

To my mind, however, the all-time low point for the Church up to now was 1976. Not only did the conflict between the two opposed camps in American Catholicism rage on then, but the confusion and division in the ranks of the American hierarchy reached dangerous new levels and became more visible than ever before, evoking the specter of schism as a plausible scenario within the larger narrative of American Catholic cultural assimilation.

As 1976 began, the nation was deeply troubled. America was less than two years removed from Richard Nixon's resignation as president in the wake of the Watergate scandal, and one year on from the fall of South Vietnam and its takeover by the communist North, after a brutal war in which 212,000 Americans were killed or wounded. The bicentennial year of American independence offered national morale an opportunity for a pick-me-up. It was a year of speeches and band concerts and parades that reached its visual peak on July 4, when a fleet of tall ships from around the world sailed majestically into New York Harbor.

Several years earlier, looking ahead to the bicentennial, the U.S. bishops' conference had set up a committee to plan the Church's official participation. John Cardinal Dearden of Detroit was named chairman, a signal that the bishops were serious about the bicentennial: as first post–Vatican II president of the National Conference of Catholic Bishops and its sister organization, the United States Catholic Conference, Cardinal Dearden enjoyed enormous prestige and influence among his fellow bishops; already he had done a great deal to shape postconciliar American Catholicism, and now he was positioned to do even more.

Staffing of the bicentennial program at the national level was entrusted to the NCCB/USCC under its general secretary, Bishop James S. Rausch, a Saint Cloud, Minnesota, priest who'd had a meteoric rise in the Church bureaucracy since coming to the bishops' conference just a few years earlier. Bishop Rausch's role in the bicentennial also was significant, since in his time as general secretary he'd emerged as an activist with no qualms about using his office to push his personal views, including an enthusiasm for liberation theology.

While the bishops' bicentennial plan had several components (both then and now, largely ignored), its much-noted centerpiece was a program that was close to the hearts of Cardinal Dearden and Bishop Rausch. Called "Liberty and Justice for All", the program was, for the cardinal, a way of reviving interest in what in the postconciliar era was usually described as "shared responsibility" for decision making in the Church; for the general secretary, the program was an instrument for promoting liberation theology.

"Liberty and Justice for All" was assembled as a national platform for social justice advocacy. Countrywide public hearings were organized, leading up to a national conference in Detroit with the name Call to Action. The purpose of all this, Cardinal Dearden explained, was to find out "how the American Catholic community can contribute to the quest of all people for liberty and justice".[34]

As this grandiose project of the Catholic Left was taking shape, a no-less-grandiose enterprise was being organized by the Archdiocese of Philadelphia: the 41st International

---

[34] Many accounts have been published of the bishops' bicentennial program, including "Liberty and Justice for All" and the Call to Action conference. Much of the present treatment is drawn from the author's personal recollections of the events and the major players involved. George A. Kelly provides a good overview and critique in *The Battle for the American Church* (Garden City, N.Y.: Image Books, 1981), 379–87. For an assessment by one of the planners, see David O'Brien, *Public Catholicism* (New York: Macmillan, 1989), 243–44.

Eucharistic Congress. This was the first of these large-scale celebrations honoring the Blessed Sacrament to be held in the United States since Cardinal Mundelein's mammoth congress in Chicago in 1926. And like Cardinal Mundelein's event and its symbolic Catholic muscle flexing, the congress in Philadelphia, while an expression of genuine devotion, was also something more than a devotional event.

Philadelphia, site of the signing of the Declaration of Independence in 1776, was an obvious location for a Eucharistic congress during the American bicentennial year. But Church observers saw another reason for the choice: John Cardinal Krol of Philadelphia wanted it. Like Detroit's Cardinal Dearden, Cardinal Krol was originally a Clevelander; and the two men's ecclesiastical careers had crisscrossed for years, creating an ambivalent, competitive relationship. After Vatican II, Cardinal Dearden was the first president of the newly organized NCCB/USCC, Cardinal Krol, younger by three years, the second president; Cardinal Dearden was the de facto leader of the hierarchy's liberal wing, Cardinal Krol of the conservatives. If Cardinal Dearden was to be patron of a left-leaning bicentennial project in Detroit, it was only natural for Cardinal Krol to respond with a bicentennial project tilting to the right in the City of Brotherly Love.

By all accounts the Eucharistic congress held in Philadelphia from August 1 to 8, 1976, with the resoundingly Catholic theme "Jesus, the Bread of Life" was a grand success. Even now, a statue depicting Jesus breaking bread stands outside Philadelphia's Cathedral Basilica of Saints Peter and Paul as a memorial of the event. The crowded program offered lectures, workshops, exhibitions, and liturgies that included an enthusiastic "Catholic youth Mass" in the Philadelphia arena called the Spectrum. Among the speakers were Karol Cardinal Wojtyla of Krakow (soon to be known to the world as Pope John Paul II); Mother Teresa of Calcutta; Dorothy Day, cofounder of the Catholic Worker; and Leo Cardinal Suenens of Belgium, a liberal star of Vatican Council II who'd become involved in the charismatic movement.

Among the speakers at the closing session was President Gerald Ford, who expressed his concern about the "growing irreverence for life" in America.[35] Three years after the Supreme Court decision in *Roe v. Wade*, abortion was a major issue in the impending presidential election. Ford understood that perfectly well, as did the pro-life Catholic audience that heard him that day in Philadelphia.

And as did others in the opposition's political camp. Four years earlier, a proabortion Democrat, George McGovern, had lost to Richard Nixon, with Nixon receiving 59% of the votes cast by Catholics. Now, in 1976, Democratic leaders were anxious to bring traditionally Democratic Catholics back to the party in the fall. Thus a quiet conversation to discuss the situation took place over breakfast at a downtown Washington club between Andrew Young, representative for former Georgia governor Jimmy Carter, by then the Democratic presidential nominee, and Bishop Rausch of the NCCB/USCC.

Their discussion led to an August 31 meeting in the capital city's historic Mayflower Hotel between Carter and the executive committee of the bishops' conference, whose members included Archbishop Joseph L. Bernardin of Cincinnati, a former general secretary who was now NCCB/USCC president; Terence Cardinal Cooke of New York,

---

[35] Quoted in "President Gerald R. Ford Brought Healing to Wounded Nation", Catholic News Service, December 27, 2006, www.catholicnews.com/data/stories/cns/0607375.htm.

chairman of the pro-life committee; and Bishop James Mal-
one of Youngstown, Ohio, a president-to-be of the bishops' conference.

Alas, the meeting did not go well. Carter told the bishops he was personally opposed to abortion. The bishops
pressed him to support a pro-life constitutional amendment. Carter demurred. Emerging from the meeting, Archbishop Bernardin said in a chaotic news conference in the
hotel lobby that he and his colleagues were "disappointed"
at the candidate's stance.

As this news spread, a firestorm of criticism for intervening in political affairs burst over the bishops' heads. This
reaction reflected the familiar double standard of the media,
who approved political activism by religious groups on behalf
of causes the media supported but condemned such activism
when the causes were ones the media opposed. Meanwhile,
believing that Carter had put his foot in it with Catholics,
Gerald Ford's staff hastened to arrange a September meeting
at the White House for the same group of bishops. Although
Ford was, in the words of a political commentator, "mushy
on abortion", he could at least point out to the NCCB/
USCC team that the Republican Party platform contained
an antiabortion plank, and could promise his support for a
constitutional amendment along the same lines. Leaving the
Oval Office, Archbishop Bernardin told the White House
press corps that the bishops were "encouraged".

This time the uproar was even louder than it had been
after the Carter meeting. The bishops were accused of trying to sway Catholics to vote for the GOP candidate. Behind
the scenes, even bishops joined in the criticism, as did other
prominent leaders in the American Church; according to
Bishop Rausch, at least four members of the episcopal conference staff threatened to resign. At a tense meeting of the

NCCB/USCC administrative committee in Washington, Archbishop Bernardin suffered through a tongue-lashing by several of his brothers and then, on September 16, 1976, held a news conference at which he issued a staff-written document showing the conference's support for Democratic policy positions and denied that the bishops harbored party or candidate preferences.

The worst year ever wore on. As fall set in, eyes turned—some in anticipation, some in dread, and most in curiosity—to Detroit, where the Call to Action conference was scheduled to take place at a downtown convention center. In more ways than one, it turned out to be a most peculiar event.

As had been promised, the preconference consultation that began in February of 1975 had been nationwide, but by no stretch of the imagination could it be called representative. A select group of about 500 people testified at hearings in Washington, D.C.; San Antonio; Minneapolis; Atlanta; Sacramento; and Newark, speaking to panels that included some bishops. Regional, diocesan, and parish meetings also took place in places that opted to have them. Although the parish events generated a seemingly impressive 800,000 responses, there was no telling how many individuals had been involved in making them, since people often put their signatures on multiple proposals. Materials assembled from these diverse sources were reviewed by eight preparatory committees charged with writing working papers and draft recommendations for the Detroit assembly.

The Call to Action conference itself drew 1,340 delegates to Detroit, but the composition of this body was no more authentically representative of American Catholicism than the preconference consultation had been. By far the larger number of delegates were named by the local bishops of 152 of the 167 American dioceses; the rest were chosen by 92 national Catholic organizations on the basis of one delegate per organization. Strange to say, the Knights of Columbus, the largest and arguably the most typical of all Catholic organizations, was not represented. Nearly a third of the delegates were priests (including 110 bishops), a little over a third were women, and half were Church employees. Conservative writer Russell Kirk, attending Call to Action as a journalist, called it an assembly of "church mice".[36]

Meeting in small groups, the delegates treated the working papers and recommendations that supposedly synthesized the preconference consultation as mere discussion starters and set to work formulating proposals of their own—for example, endorsing the proposed Equal Rights Amendment to the Constitution, which the American bishops were eventually to oppose on the grounds that it would guarantee a right to abortion.

In all, the 29 general recommendations were divided into 218 separate items. While the intervening years have dulled the proposals' impact now, observers at the time found many radical by the standards of that day, especially coming from a group of Catholics convened under the auspices of the American bishops. Proposals included returning laicized priests to ministry, ordaining women and married men, permitting lay preaching, allowing the use of contraception, adopting an open attitude toward homosexuality, and giving Holy Communion to divorced and remarried Catholics whose first unions hadn't been declared null by the Church. Recommendations on social and political issues supported amnesty for Vietnam War resisters and for undocumented immigrants, along with much else.

[36] Russell Kirk, *The Sword of Imagination: Memoirs of a Half-Century of Literary Conflict* (Grand Rapids, Mich.: Eerdmans, 1995), 427.

This wasn't what many of the bishops had expected. As a group of us waited outside our hotel for a bus to the Detroit airport, one unhappy member of the American hierarchy approached me and demanded, "Why do you people in Washington make these things happen?"

To which I could only reply, "Why do you bishops let them happen?"

Officially, the bishops received the Call to Action recommendations with thanks. An ad hoc NCCB/USCC committee was created to look into implementing them. Not much came of it.

Capping off the worst year was an ugly fight within the bishops' conference over a now-forgotten pastoral letter called *To Live in Christ Jesus*. The bishops debated this document heatedly and finally adopted it at their general meeting in November of 1976. Its genesis was as follows.

Several years earlier, the episcopal conference had published a surprisingly well-received statement on moral values in the United States. Emboldened by that success, the bishops opted for the writing of a collective pastoral letter on morality that would have the heightened stature of such a document. Since Auxiliary Bishop John B. McDowell of Pittsburgh, nationally known in Catholic education circles, had headed the group responsible for the earlier statement, he was the logical choice to chair the drafting committee for the pastoral letter. And since I had done the drafting of that statement, I was assigned to work with the new McDowell committee on the pastoral letter. I recruited Dr. William E. May, a moral theologian who then taught at the Catholic University of America and later at the John Paul II Institute for Studies on Marriage and Family, to serve as theological consultant and chief writer.

The committee, in going about its work, conducted an extensive consultation focused especially on practitioners in the fields of moral theology and ethics. Hundreds of documents poured in offering suggestions and insights. Some of these were well thought out and helpful; others were disturbingly symptomatic of the confusion and dissent existing in the ranks of people who supposedly were specialists in these disciplines.

As time passed, it became clear that Bishop McDowell, while desiring that the pastoral letter be as truly "pastoral" as possible, had no intention of using that as camouflage for a document that undermined Church teaching on matters like contraception and homosexual acts. As this realization spread, some bishops and NCCB/USCC staff set out to torpedo the project. Their efforts came to a head shortly before the general meeting at which the pastoral letter was to be debated and, presumably, adopted. Several of my colleagues at the episcopal conference arranged privately for an outside theologian to write an "alternative" text that would take the place of the one being prepared under Bishop McDowell's supervision. I was instructed to send this "alternative" to the members of the McDowell committee—behind the committee chairman's back—for their anticipated approval.

But my instructions had a loophole: Do that if you think best. As it happened, I didn't think it best. The alternative pastoral was ambiguous about contraception and homosexual acts, a not-terribly-subtle attempt to undercut Church teaching without flatly denying it. Told to do what I thought was best, I sent the committee the text that Dr. May had drafted and I had polished. This, then, was the version that the bishops' general assembly had before it when it convened.

On the floor of the meeting, the draft ran into heavy, and seemingly stage-managed, opposition from members of the hierarchy who complained that it wasn't "pastoral" enough—that is, it said too clearly that contraception and homosexual acts are wrong. One of them suggested returning the document to committee for more work, which everyone knew would be a way of killing it. Bishop McDowell was having none of that. If this product of a two-year effort to say what the Catholic Church believes about morality isn't acceptable, he told the bishops, they could find another chairman. Sensing that there would be no volunteers for the job, the American bishops dropped the subject and approved the draft, though with an unusually strong negative vote.

"But the damage was done", conservative Catholic activist Monsignor George A. Kelly later wrote. "The specter of bishops wavering uncertainly over Catholic moral values, of bishops meeting in caucus to obstruct a carefully prepared document of the National Conference, was not an image conducive to engendering confidence among those asked to live with Jesus in the manner prescribed by the bishops." [37] No doubt. Yet in the end *To Live in Christ Jesus* did hold the line on essentials of Catholic moral teaching at a critical moment. Shocking as the engineered opposition to the pastoral letter had been, it would have been worse if the document had gone down in defeat.

As 1976 drew to a close, attention shifted to Memphis, Tennessee. There on December 5, defying orders from Rome, the local ordinary, Bishop Carroll Dozier, held a penance service in the Mid-South Coliseum in Memphis conferring general absolution upon 11,500 people. General

[37] Kelly, *Battle*, 358.

absolution—the forgiving of sins without private, personal confession to a priest—is permitted by the Catholic Church in emergency situations; battlefield conditions are the classic example. In the years after Vatican II, however, the practice had begun to crop up here and there as a way of giving absolution to groups of people who, for whatever reason or reasons, just didn't care to confess their sins. The Memphis rite raised this absolution-en-masse to new heights.

Many people knew by then that 1976 had been a difficult year for the Church, and the future didn't look much better. What they could not know was that in less than two years Cardinal Karol Wojtyla of Krakow would be elected pope and, taking the name John Paul II, would launch the Church on her long slog back from the brink. "Be not afraid", John Paul urged the people of God. The events of 1976, the worst year ever, supply a permanent answer to the obvious question: "Afraid of what?"

4. Catholic Higher Education

On the eve of a July 2009 meeting in Rome between U.S. President Barack Obama and Pope Benedict XVI, Kathleen Kennedy Townsend posted a comment on the *Newsweek* blog. Townsend—daughter of Robert Kennedy, niece of John F. Kennedy, former lieutenant governor of Maryland, and a Democratic Party stalwart—began like this:

> Tomorrow Pope Benedict XVI and President Barack Obama meet for the first time, an affair much anticipated and in some circles frowned upon by American Catholics in the wake of Obama's controversial Notre Dame commencement speech in May. Conservatives in the church denounced Obama's appearance as a nod by the premier Catholic

university to a conciliatory politics that heralds the start of a slippery moral slope.

In truth, though, Obama's pragmatic approach to divisive policy (his notion that we should acknowledge the good faith underlying opposing viewpoints) and his social-justice agenda reflect the views of American Catholic laity much more closely than those of vocal bishops and pro-life activists. When Obama meets the pope tomorrow, they'll politely disagree about reproductive freedoms and homosexuality, but Catholics back home won't care, because they know Obama's on their side. In fact, Obama's agenda is closer to their views than even the pope's.[38]

A subhead read, "Why Barack Obama represents American Catholics better than the pope does".

Townsend no doubt intended her comments to be provocative, and provocative they certainly were. But some Catholic readers found her words disturbing for other reasons. Preeminent among these was that fact that although traditional Catholics wouldn't have agreed that President Obama represented their views better than the pope did, a substantial number of Catholics more or less alienated from the Church may very well have responded, "She's right."

And, as Townsend pointed out, the battle lines between opposed groups of Catholics had been drawn with great clarity earlier in the year in the course of a notable controversy surrounding the University of Notre Dame's decision to invite Obama to be its commencement speaker in May 2009 and receive an honorary degree. The furor centered on the fact that Obama was unabashedly pro-choice on abortion and strongly committed to the defense and

---

[38] "Without a Doubt: Why Barack Obama Represents American Catholics Better than the Pope Does", Daily Beast, July 8, 2009, http://www.thedailybeast.com/newsweek/2009/07/08/without-a-doubt.html.

promotion of the abortion "right" as an important policy position of his administration.[39]

This, though, is not just the story of a single university and a single president. The Notre Dame–Obama affair was a paradigm of an ongoing debate over the Catholic identity of Catholic colleges and universities in America.

Founded in 1842 by French priests of the Congregation of Holy Cross, the University of Notre Dame du Lac occupies an iconic place in American Catholicism. The campus itself broadcasts the fact that here is a very special institution. The last time I strolled there, under a deep blue June sky glowing with crystalline splendor, I made a surprising discovery: at Notre Dame, even the trees have donor plaques.

Now, there's nothing intrinsically wrong with a school using its trees to raise money—it's much the same as parish and parochial school bake sales and raffles, just more sophisticated. But this creative use of its trees does express the particular genius that prevails at Notre Dame: Only God can make a tree, but this is a school that makes money

---

[39] The president's position was spelled out yet again in a statement released by the White House on January 22, 2011, to mark the 38th anniversary of *Roe v. Wade* and *Doe v. Bolton*, the 1973 Supreme Court decisions legalizing abortion in the United States: "Today marks the 38th anniversary of *Roe v. Wade*, the Supreme Court decision that protects women's health and reproductive freedom, and affirms a fundamental principle: that government should not intrude on private family matters. I am committed to protecting this constitutional right. I also remain committed to policies, initiatives, and programs that help prevent unintended pregnancies, support women and mothers, encourage healthy relationships, and promote adoption. And on this anniversary, I hope that we will recommit ourselves more broadly to ensuring that our daughters have the same rights, the same freedoms, and the same opportunities as our sons to fulfill their dreams." The statement did not say how many American daughters dream of having abortions. "Statement by the President on Roe v. Wade Anniversary", January 22, 2011, www.whitehouse.gov/the-press-office?2011/01/22/statement-president-roe-v-wade.

from the shrubbery. It's American to the *n*th degree, with that special get-up-and-go brand of Americanism that people like H. L. Mencken and Sinclair Lewis gleefully skewered in their day.

It also was the spirit of Americanism discernible in Notre Dame's invitation to Obama—"a coup", pronounced Kenneth Woodward, a former *Newsweek* religion editor who is a Notre Dame alumnus and a longtime booster of his old school. Perhaps it was; but a coup on behalf of what? That was the crux of the controversy that followed the invitation.

Notre Dame's many defenders argued that universities are rightly open to hearing diverse points of view. But Obama wasn't asked just to give a lecture—he was invited to receive the highest honor Notre Dame can bestow. Outrageous, the critics said. But what if it was? Notre Dame is an important university in the American academic manner. Notre Dame could jolly well do whatever it pleased.

In the end, more than 300,000 people signed a protest petition, and over 80 American bishops took the unusual step of speaking out individually—many in decidedly harsh tones—in criticism of the university. Sean Cardinal O'Malley of Boston declined to accept an honorary degree from Notre Dame at the same time Obama got his. Apparently recognizing that it had ventured onto thin ice, Notre Dame since then has taken visible steps to bolster its pro-life credentials and promote its identity as a Catholic institution, including dropping charges—two years after the fact—against a number of pro-lifers who'd been arrested after they invaded the campus to protest Obama's presence at the commencement.

In the feature mentioned earlier assessing colleges and universities, the journal *First Things* said this about Notre Dame: "Let's say a word on her behalf. Notre Dame's student body reflects the American Catholic Church in all its glory, as does the university as a whole. In some ways, it is clearly a school in decline: The philosophy department, the administration, and the sports program are all decaying. Still, Notre Dame remains a decidedly Catholic institution." [40]

Of the assessment of the school as Catholic, a student wrote: "It depends on the class and the professor." At Notre Dame, it seems, you can get pretty much whatever you want, whether it's High Catholicism or standard secularism. Like other American Catholic universities, Notre Dame has changed tremendously over the years. Whether for better or for worse depends largely on which area or areas of its institutional ethos one has in view. Many people are well pleased with Notre Dame as it is now, but Charles E. Rice, an emeritus law professor, speaks of "four decades of erosion".[41]

In the introduction to a book by Rice about the Obama affair, Alfred J. Freddoso, a veteran professor of philosophy at Notre Dame, explained the university's special place in the American Catholic imagination and the relevance that has to the Obama invitation. During the first six decades of the twentieth century, he wrote, Notre Dame's success, "especially on the football field, was symbolic of the aspirations of hundreds of thousands of Catholic immigrants who were struggling to 'make it' in America".[42] During the 1950s, though, the university undertook a major effort to shed its image as a football school and become a distinguished institution of higher learning. The crucial turning point in this

[40] "Degrees of Faith: A *First Things* Survey of America's Colleges and Universities", *First Things*, November 2010.
[41] Charles E. Rice, *What Happened to Notre Dame?* (South Bend, Ind.: St. Augustine's Press, 2009), 154.
[42] Alfred J. Freddoso, "Introduction", in ibid., xix.

evolutionary process came in the early 1970s: a "gamble" by the Notre Dame administration, following Vatican II and the dissent from *Humanae vitae*, on the proposition that "some form of 'liberal' or 'progressive' Catholicism, freed from (or, more neutrally, disengaged from) the philosophical and theological underpinnings of the past, would emerge as the 'serious' Catholicism of the future."[43]

> Perhaps at the time this did not seem like much of a gamble. After all, a significant percentage of American bishops, along with their closest advisors, seemed perfectly comfortable with progressive agendas. In any case, at Notre Dame the attitude of dissent from and disdain for the Vatican played a significant foundational role in shaping hiring policies, tenure decisions, key administrative appointments, curricular reform, and admissions strategies for the next thirty years.[44]

From the standpoint of those making the gamble, it paid off. In recent decades, Freddoso concluded, the school and its graduates both have "made it big if we concentrate merely on material success". Quite naturally, then, "many American Catholics—perhaps a majority, including a majority of Notre Dame alumni—were undoubtedly pleased to hear that the newly inaugurated President of the United States would be visiting Notre Dame to get an honorary degree."[45]

For many years the guiding spirit in the evolution of Notre Dame was Father Theodore M. Hesburgh, C.S.C., president of the university from 1952 to 1987. George Kelly describes him as "in the vanguard of those Catholics who

[43] Ibid., xxi.
[44] Ibid.
[45] Ibid., xix.

wish to redefine the Catholic university and perhaps to redefine the Catholic Church, too".[46] A critical moment in the process of redefinition occurred in July of 1967 at a Notre Dame conference center in northern Wisconsin called Land O' Lakes.

Recall that in 1955 Monsignor John Tracy Ellis had rocked the small world of American Catholic academe by pointing to the weaknesses of Catholic schools. Monsignor Ellis called on their leaders to adopt the standards of the secular academic establishment in order to be accepted there, much as anxious high school seniors shape their admissions essays with an eye to pleasing college admissions officers. Twelve years later, 26 representatives of seven Catholic universities, nearly all of them priests, gathered at Land O' Lakes for a key step in the direction pointed by Ellis and others. The schools represented, besides Notre Dame, were Boston College, the Catholic University of America, Fordham, Georgetown, Saint Louis, and Seton Hall. The result was the famous Land O' Lakes Document, a declaration of less than 2,000 words that set not only the signers' own institutions but most of the rest of American Catholic higher education on a problematic new path. The document began this way:

> The Catholic university today must be a university in the full modern sense of the word, with a strong commitment to and concern for academic excellence. To perform its teaching and research function effectively the Catholic university must have a true autonomy and academic freedom in the face of authority of whatever kind, lay or clerical, external to the academic community itself. To say this is simply to assert that institutional autonomy and academic freedom are

[46] Kelly, *Battle*, 82.

essential conditions for life and growth and indeed of sur-
vival for Catholic universities as for all universities.[47]

The distinctiveness of such institutions is said to lie in this:
"The Catholic university must be an institution, a community of learners or a community of scholars, in which Catholicism is perceptively present and effectively operative."[48]

Quite soon, Kelly recalls, this document became "the
'right' position for leading spokesmen of Catholic higher
education".[49] As its critics point out, the ideal it seemingly
proposes—the university's autonomy in the face of external
authority of whatever kind—is neither attainable nor even
desirable. Universities are necessarily accountable to external authorities of many sorts, among them accrediting agencies and the local, state, and federal governments. No
reasonable person, including no one in the university world,
objects to that. But the framers of the Land O' Lakes Document weren't thinking of autonomy in relation to these
external bodies. They were declaring the autonomy of their
schools in a special sense: in relation to the teaching and
governing authority of the Catholic Church. Thus understood, the thrust of their declaration is that it's up to the
people running a Catholic school, and nobody else, to decide
what counts as Catholicism's "perceptive presence" and
"effective operation" on that particular campus.

In 1990 Pope John Paul II published a document called
Ex corde Ecclesiae (From the heart of the Church), which
sets out principles to guide the relationship between Catholic higher education and the ecclesial community. It too

---

[47] Quoted in ibid., 64.

[48] Land O' Lakes Document, quoted in George A. Kelly, *The Battle for the American Church* (Garden City, N.Y.: Doubleday, 1979), 64.

[49] Ibid.

extols institutional autonomy and academic freedom, though with a significant condition attached: "so long as the rights of the individual person and of the community are preserved within the confines of the truth and the common good".[50] Declaring it the purpose of a Catholic university to ensure an institutional Christian presence in the world of higher learning, *Ex corde Ecclesiae* identifies four "essential characteristics" of such a school. These are a "Christian inspiration" both of individuals and of the university community as a whole; continuing reflection in the light of faith upon the growing body of human knowledge; "fidelity to the Christian message as it comes to us through the Church"; and commitment to the service of the Church and the human family.[51]

The bishops of the United States, after trying for a decade, in 1999, finally succeeded in adopting and promulgating a document acceptable to Rome that applied the principles of *Ex corde Ecclesiae* to Catholic higher education in America.[52] In January 2011 the U.S. Conference of Catholic Bishops announced plans for a review of how the implementation had worked. Developed in collaboration with university representatives, the plan was for bishops to meet individually with presidents of Catholic colleges and universities in their dioceses, then discuss the results among themselves at their general assembly in November of the same year.

"Dialogue between bishop and president provides an important means to foster a mutually beneficial relationship",

---

[50] John Paul II, *Ex corde Ecclesiae*, nos. 12 (Falls Church, Va.: The Cardinal Newman Society, 1990).

[51] Ibid., no. 14.

[52] National Conference of Catholic Bishops, "*Ex Corde Ecclesiae*: An Application to the United States", November 19, 1999, www.catholicculture.org/culture/library/view.cfm?recn.

the bishop-chairman of the USCCB education committee observed. It would be impossible to quarrel with that. But in the years since Land O' Lakes, the Catholic identity of many American Catholic colleges and universities has been compromised. This represents a serious loss for the Church, which needs the collaboration of integrally Catholic institutions of higher learning in order to confront (in Pope John Paul II's words) "the great problems of society and culture".[53]

As this is written, the need to defend academic freedom on the Catholic campus against the inroads of the Magisterium no longer seems as pressing as it may have appeared to people in Catholic higher education in the 1960s and 1970s. According to the president of the Catholic University of America, John H. Garvey, nearly 50 years after Land O' Lakes, academic freedom is secure: "What we need to worry about is, 'Where's the beef?'"[54]

The quashing of Catholic identity on many Catholic campuses has continued despite *Ex corde Ecclesiae* and the U.S. bishops' document on its application. The University of Notre Dame is a high-visibility, high-prestige case in point. Notre Dame makes much of its Catholic identity, but critics inside and outside the university point to policies and repeated actions in contradiction to that. Can dialogue reverse what already has happened? In the absence of a serious rethinking of Land O' Lakes, we're not likely to find out.

Oh, and Obama at Notre Dame? The president delivered a largely anodyne commencement talk that nevertheless did contain at least one very odd passage. This section

[53] *Ex corde Ecclesiae*, no. 13.
[54] "Fostering American Catholic Intellectual Life", an interview by the author with John H. Garvey published in the September 4, 2011, issue of *Our Sunday Visitor*.

of the speech began with a materialistic account of faith, which Obama said "necessarily admits doubt" because it is "the belief in things not seen".[55] On this basis, he proceeded to urge the graduates of a major Catholic university not to believe with certainty anything having to do with religion. Approaching faith in this agnostic manner has practical consequences, he said: "This doubt ... should temper our passions, and cause us to be wary of self-righteousness.... And within our vast democracy, this doubt should remind us to persuade through reason, through an appeal whenever we can to universal rather than parochial principles." [56] As protestors demonstrated to protest Obama's presence, the big crowd ate it up.

5. Sex Abuse, Clericalism, and Secrecy

It's easy to perceive a special American dimension in many of the problems facing the Church in the United States in the early years of the twenty-first century. Theological dissent, the public repudiation of Catholic teaching by Catholic politicians and public figures, the vanishing Catholic identity of Catholic colleges and universities—all have a special American coloration here. It would be difficult, though, to make the same claim regarding the sexual abuse of children by priests and its cover-up by Church authorities. As we've learned more about abuse and cover-up elsewhere—in Canada, Ireland, Germany, Great Britain, Holland, Belgium, and other countries—we find that the substance of

[55] "Remarks made by the President in Commencement Address at the University of Notre Dame", May 17, 2009, Whitehouse Office of the Press Secretary, www.whitehouse.gov/the-press-office/remarks-president-notre-dame-commencement.
[56] Ibid.

the scandal has appeared to be very much the same wherever it occurs.

So why even mention it in a book about the Americanization of American Catholicism? The answer, quite simply, is that no treatment of problems facing the Church in the United States today can avoid speaking about clergy sex abuse and cover-up, and about the two factors that did so much to create and perpetuate this horrible scandal—clericalism and the abuse of secrecy.

A friend whose love for and loyalty to the Church are well beyond the ordinary tells a story dating back to the early days of this ugly affair that deserves to be pondered for what it says about the scandal's roots.

In the mid-1980s, after clerical sex abuse had come to light for the first time in a case from Lafayette, Louisiana, my friend and some other laypeople were discussing the shocking revelations with several priests. All of them, priests and laity, were staunch Catholics devoted to the Church.

Without exception, my friend recalls, the clerics took the view that a priest guilty of sexually abusing a minor "should be sent off for treatment and put back into some kind of service—at least, restricted service or some kind of low-level administrative job". At the time, it should be added, this was a defensible view, since even mental health professionals hadn't yet grasped that the propensity to engage in child sexual abuse was a nearly untreatable condition. But all of the laypeople present nevertheless considered it a bad idea, with my friend arguing that if a priest was guilty even once of abusing a child, "he should be *out*, since such acts are a gross betrayal of the laity's trust."

"But", he adds, recalling the incident, "all of the priests tended to be more concerned with the erring cleric. Those were good priests too. But they were imbued with a clericalist mentality—very much as those good plantation owners in the pre–Civil War South who treated their slaves well were imbued with racism." Since then, this same point has been made repeatedly by many others: the fundamental mistake of bishops and superiors who hushed up the crimes of priests, sent them for brief stays in therapy centers, and then gave them new pastoral assignments without telling anyone about their history arose from concentrating on what supposedly would be best for the priests, with little regard for those the priests had victimized or might victimize in the future. In other words, it arose from clericalism. As researchers from the John Jay College of Criminal Justice concluded in their study of the "causes and context" of clergy sex abuse, "the response [of diocesan authorities] typically focused on the priest-abusers rather than on the victims. . . . The majority of diocesan leaders took actions to help 'rehabilitate' the abusive priests." [57]

In a way, that wasn't new. Clericalism in the Catholic Church is like the pattern in the wallpaper: it's been there so long that you don't see it anymore. This may be why, amid new policies and structures and procedures put in place in 2002 by the American bishops in response to disclosures that bishops in a number of dioceses had covered up cases of abuse, little was said, and less done, about clericalism and the need to eliminate it once and for all from the life of the Church. Yet clericalism and the clericalist mentality were at the heart of this noxious episode, just as they are at the heart of many other ecclesiastical problems and abuses.

Clericalism doesn't cause sex abuse, any more than sex abuse causes clericalism. But when sex abuse occurs in a clericalized setting, such as a typical parish, the situation

---

[57] *Causes and Context*, 4.

takes on a distinctly clericalist hue. As the facts of this scandal have come to light, it's become clear that, in combination with other mistaken attitudes and ways of acting, the attitudes and ways associated with clericalism usually played a large part in the response when a priest was found to have engaged in abuse: his bishop and other clerics hushed up what had happened (to prevent scandal, it was said), shielded and sequestered the offender, and in general behaved like members of an exclusive club anxious to protect erring fellow members and preserve the club's good image. In this way a tragedy for individuals became a world-class disaster for the Church.

The sexual abuse of children is often said to be linked to power. Clericalism is similarly linked. At the start, generosity moves men to pursue a calling to the priesthood; but in some, it seems, the generous impulse comes to be corrupted by a growing taste for the pleasures of unearned authority. "Probably in no other walk of life", remarks the priest-narrator in Edwin O'Connor's novel *The Edge of Sadness*, "is a young man so often and so humbly approached by his elders and asked for his advice." [58] Such deference can be an exceedingly dangerous trap.

Clericalism and sex abuse also are related to the abuse of secrecy. The National Review Board, an all-lay body established by the American bishops to monitor the implementation of their policy on preventing and punishing sex abuse, makes this point:

> Clerical culture and a misplaced sense of loyalty made some priests look the other way.... Clericalism also contributed to a culture of secrecy. In many instances, Church leaders

[58] Edwin O'Connor, *The Edge of Sadness* (Boston: Little, Brown, 1961), 119.

valued confidentiality and a priest's right to privacy above the prevention of further harm to victims.... [C]hurch leaders kept information from parishioners and other dioceses that should have been provided to them. Some also pressured victims not to inform the authorities or the public of abuse.[59]

The us-versus-them world view characteristic of a self-protective managerial class easily leads to corruption and to the abuse of secrecy. Ethicist Sissela Bok writes:

"Every aspect of the shared predicament influences the secret practice over time: in particular, the impediments to reasoning and to choice, and the limitations on sympathy and on regard for human beings. The tendency to view the world in terms of insiders and outsiders can then build up a momentum that it would lack if it were short-lived and immediately accountable."[60]

Bok is not speaking specifically of clergy sex abuse, but her words describe it well.

In a canonical study of the scandal as it took shape prior to the revelations of 2002, Nicholas P. Cafardi, emeritus

[59] National Review Board for the Protection of Children and Young People, *A Report on the Crisis in the Catholic Church in the United States*, in *Origins*, March 11, 2004.

[60] Sissela Bok, *Secrets: On the Ethics of Concealment and Revelation* (New York: Vintage Books, 1983), 110. In writing my book *Nothing to Hide: Secrecy, Communication and Communion in the Catholic Church* (San Francisco: Ignatius Press, 2008), I found the insights of Bok, a non-Catholic, extremely helpful. Unfortunately, I found little that was helpful in the work of most Catholic moralists, who typically discuss truth telling and secrecy in relation to the permissibility of lying and withholding the truth. Up to this time, it seems not to have occurred to them that serious harm is done to the Church when people in authority, unreasonably pleading confidentiality, fail to provide other Catholics with information they need to function as informed, responsible, engaged members of the ecclesial community.

dean of the Duquesne University law school and one of the National Review Board's original members, includes the following among the scandal's lessons: "[N]o legal system or system of governance can be effective when its highest value is secrecy." Citing chapter and verse to show how attachment to what proved to be an ultimately illusory secrecy crippled Church authorities in their efforts to face up to this grave crisis, Cafardi concludes on this passionate note: "Avoiding scandal is simply not a valid excuse for secrecy and a lack of accountability.... The idea that secrecy should be a value, let alone a foundational one, in Christ's Church, its legal system, or its system of governance should be abhorrent. Secrecy is the enemy of openness and truth."[61]

Many people expected that a big drop in Mass attendance would follow the disclosures of 2002, but it didn't. The percentage of Catholics regularly attending Sunday Mass remained stable throughout the decade that followed, hovering in the 22%–25% range. That figure is hardly something to take much comfort in, but at least the scandal didn't make it worse. It appears that faithful Catholics know how to distinguish between the weakness of Church members, including both the leaders and themselves, and the core of essential goodness and truth at the heart of the Church.

The situation is not the same for the bishops, however. Like people who think well of their own congressman but don't like Congress, Catholics similarly tend to take a positive view of their local bishop while viewing "the bishops" in a negative light. A Zogby poll in 2010 found only 45% of American Catholics approving of the overall job

---

[61] Nicholas P. Cafardi, *Before Dallas: The U.S. Bishops' Response to Clergy Sexual Abuse of Children* (Mahwah, N.J.: Paulist Press, 2008), 154.

the bishops were doing, and 72% having a negative view of the bishops' handling of sex abuse.[62]

While this clearly means that today's bishops are paying, to some extent, for the mistakes of their predecessors, it also may point to something else: an unmet need for today's bishops to get serious about things that sooner or later could erode even the patience of faithful Catholics—clericalism and the abuse of secrecy.

We shall return to these matters below when discussing the reform of American Catholicism. Against the background sketched here, however, another question comes first: Where has the Americanization project in American Catholicism taken us? The first section of the chapter that follows will examine the troubling answer to that question at length.

[62] John Zogby, "The Catholic Church: A Failed Institution?", May 6, 2010, www.huffington.post.com/john-zogby/the-catholic-church-a-fai_b_566344.html.

4

"THE FAITH OF OUR FATHERS"

Who is left among you that saw this house in its former
glory? How do you see it now? Is it not in your sight as
nothing? Yet now take courage, O Zerubbabel, says the
LORD; take courage, O Joshua, son of Jehozadak, the high
priest; take courage, all you people of the land, says the
LORD; work, for I am with you, says the LORD of hosts,
according to the promise that I made you when you came
out of Egypt.

—Haggai 2:3–5

A historian of Boston Catholicism presents this picture of
how things were in the years after World War II:

After the war, Catholic life in most parishes moved along
old familiar paths, continuing to offer its adherents an active
and fulfilling spiritual life. And the congregations responded
with eagerness and enthusiasm. During the late 1940s and
early 1950s, Catholic churches were still filled to overflow-
ing at each Mass on Sundays and Holy Days of Obligation;
parishioners went to confession every Saturday night; the
altar rails were crowded with communicants every Sunday
morning. . . . Old people and young people trudged through
the snow on cold February mornings during Lent to attend
early morning Mass. . . . During the 1940s and 1950s,
societies and associations that had first started under

173

Archbishop Williams and then expanded remarkably under Cardinal O'Connell took on new size and vigor under Cushing. . . .

And there were signs that this growth and vitality would continue well into the future. Returning veterans had already started their families, had their children baptized in the Catholic Church, and were beginning to send these children into the local parochial schools, which were expanding at a phenomenal rate under the archbishop's energetic building program.[1]

It is a remarkable fact that between 1944 and 1960, the Catholic population of the Archdiocese of Boston rose 250,000–300,000 every five years.

Another author, writing in 2008, gives a profoundly different picture of Catholicism in Boston as it had become by then:

The Boston archdiocese has sharply contracted, giving back the gains of the past generation. . . . There are more Catholics in Greater Boston (in absolute terms) than there were a generation ago. But the affluent young Catholics of the early twenty-first century have not been visiting their parishes often enough, or tossing enough money in the collection baskets, to pay the heating bills on churches that their working-class ancestors sacrificed to build . . . The corps of clergy is aging as well as shrinking. . . . [I]n 2004 there were 130 parishes with a pastor above the age of seventy. . . . Catholics divorce and remarry, obtain abortions and sterilizations, use birth control and *in vitro* fertilization, all at rates indistinguishable from those of their non-Catholic neighbors. In the mid-twentieth century Catholics had established their

---

[1] Thomas H. O'Connor, *Boston Catholics: A History of the Church and Its People* (Boston: Northeastern University Press, 1998), 247–49.

own distinct culture in Boston. . . . Now somehow that culture has dissipated.[2]

Boston is hardly alone. Making allowance for local variations, the same situation exists in Catholic dioceses throughout the United States.

In 2008 the Pew Forum on Religion and Public Life, a
major American religious research institution, shook up the
church world with findings of what it called a "Religious
Landscape Survey". Based on interviews with 35,000 adults,
the survey showed that nearly half of all Americans have
either changed religion one or more times or else have
entirely dropped out of organized religion.

Catholic commentators had particular reason for viewing the Pew data with dismay. The Pew Forum reported
that there were 22 million ex-Catholics in the United States,
meaning that one out of every three Americans who'd been
raised Catholic had left the Church. "One in three",
marveled Peter Steinfels, an old-line liberal Catholic who is
former editor of *Commonweal* and former chief religion writer
of the *New York Times*. "Think about it. This record makes
the percentage of bad loans and mortgages leading to the
financial meltdown look absolutely stellar." [3]

Some time after the release of these findings, the Pew
Forum's director, Luis Lugo, sought to soften the blow
in an interview with John Allen of the *National Catholic
Reporter*. "Everybody's losing members in this country, some
even more than Catholics", he said. "In percentage terms,

---

[2] Philip F. Lawler, *The Faithful Departed: The Collapse of Boston's Catholic
Culture* (New York: Encounter Books, 2008), 3–4.

[3] Peter Steinfels, "Further Adrift", *Commonweal*, October 22, 2010,
http://www.commonwealmagazine.org/further-adrift.

Catholic losses are not out of line with other groups." This was rather as if one passenger on the Titanic were to tell another, "Don't feel bad; everyone's in the same boat."

Nevertheless, Lugo conceded that the Catholic Church in America does have a serious problem peculiar to itself:

> "It's on the recruitment side that Catholics are not doing as well. Protestants are losing lots of members too, but for every four Americans who are no longer Protestant, there are three who are Protestant today who were not raised that way. Protestantism is declining as a whole but the recruitment rate is pretty good. Catholics are not replenishing their ranks through conversion in the same way."

Hispanic immigration and higher-than-average fertility rates among Hispanic Catholics explain why the Catholic numbers weren't worse. Lugo said: "If the only factor driving a religious group's share of the population were conversion, the Catholic church would be declining." [4]

Apparently too the problem isn't only that the Catholic Church isn't getting her share of converts by comparison with Protestant bodies; rather, the number of Catholic conversions also is dropping. Some casually assembled figures of my own, drawn from the *Official Catholic Directory*, show that Catholic conversions in 2000 numbered 178,533 ("adult baptisms" and "received into full communion" combined) and in 2010 had fallen to 119,003. That is a decline of nearly 60,000 in 10 years.

"I realize that I am grieving", Peter Steinfels writes. The grief is probably widely shared among serious Catholics. In Steinfels' case and that of many others, it focuses on the

---

[4] John L. Allen Jr., "In America's Religious Marketplace, the Real Catholic Problem Is New Sales", *National Catholic Reporter*, February 11, 2011, http://ncronline.org/blogs/all-things-catholic/americas-religious-marketplace-real-catholic-problem-new-sales.

prospect that the "priceless blessing" of the faith may not be present in his grandchildren's lives. Some Catholics, however, have passed beyond grieving and the anger that underlies it, and reached a state of

> "resignation to either a death of faith or withdrawal from the church. For others, it means the impossibility of being in any way a 'public Catholic,' whether in their fields of work, their communities, their parishes, or their circles of family and friends. Pray, receive the sacraments, button one's lips." [5]

Rhetoric aside, how bad, really, is the situation as it pertains to those who—up to now at least—haven't formally quit the Church? The numbers give a picture of a religious body in which what used to be a crisis has become decline.[6]

But before we look at those numbers, a disclaimer is needed. Numbers don't get to the essentials of faith—the action of grace, the response of human freedom, the quiet revolutions worked by sanctity in individual lives and, sometimes, in the larger community. Usually these things take

---

[5] Steinfels, "Further Adrift".

[6] Not everyone sees it that way, of course. For example, James Davidson, a Purdue University emeritus professor of sociology who has done many studies of American Catholics over the years, distinguishes between former Catholics who have joined other religious bodies and most likely will not return to the Catholic Church, and those who have left but remained unaffiliated and may still be counted as having some sort of relationship with the Church. "Many of the so-called 'unaffiliated' are still 'family.' They may be distant cousins, but they are far more accessible than those who have joined some other faith." Thus, Davidson concludes, "the church may not be hemorrhaging quite as badly as some reports suggest." Perhaps not; but Church leaders would hardly be acting responsibly if they were to frame pastoral strategies on the supposition that people who do not accept the Church's teaching and governing authority or share in her sacramental life nevertheless continue to have a meaningful relationship with her. They do not, and the Church had best face that fact. See James Davidson, "Twenty-Somethings: The Known and the Unknown", *Origins*, March 3, 2011.

place beyond the reach of counting and quantifying. Still, the numbers are important as signs pointing to inner realities with spiritual significance. They do not tell us everything, but they do tell us things we need to know.

Here, then, are some of the American Catholic numbers as they look today.

According to the *Official Catholic Directory* for 2011 (reporting data for 2010), Catholics in the United States numbered 68,503,456.[7] That was 388,000 more than the year before and an increase of 6 million during the preceding decade. It also was about 22.1% of the total population. By no means, though, are Catholics evenly distributed through the 50 states, nor are they a geographically static body. A survey by the Program on Public Values at Trinity College in Hartford concluded that, largely as a result of immigration, by 2008 the Catholic share of the total population had risen by a third in California and Texas and by a fourth in Florida; but in the Northeast, a traditional Catholic bastion, the Catholic share of the population had dropped from 46% to 36%. In Rhode Island, long the most heavily Catholic state in the nation, the percentage of Catholics declined from 62% to 46%; in New York, it declined from 44% to 37%, with an overall loss of 800,000.

During the last half century, stunning changes have occurred among priests, religious sisters, and religious brothers.

In 1965, the year Vatican Council II ended, priests in the United States numbered 58,632. That figure included 35,925 diocesan priests and 22,707 religious order priests. By 2010 the total was 40,788, including 27,614 diocesan priests and

---

[7] The Center for Applied Research in the Apostolate believes that the real number is some nine or ten million higher. The difference reflects a difference in methodologies. I used the *Directory* figure here because I am also using its figures for other categories and other years.

13,174 religious priests (but not including American priests with overseas assignments). In 1965 there were 994 priestly ordinations and 8,325 graduate-level seminarians. The 2010 figures were 472 ordinations and 5,131 seminarians (3,319 diocesan, 1,812 religious). The reinstitution of the order of permanent deacon after Vatican II (17,165 deacons in 2010) and the emergence of lay ecclesial ministers since the 1970s (now about 35,000) has helped soften the blow in parishes and other church institutions, but in no way does it alter the fact that the number of priests has fallen drastically and is continuing to drop.

Declines among sisters and brothers have even been steeper. Religious women numbered almost 180,000 in 1965 and 58,724 in 2010; figures for religious brothers were 12,271 and 4,735 respectively. In 2010 there were more American sisters over the age of 90 than under the age of 60. Some communities of religious women—generally, those described as "traditional"—are growing, although in absolute numbers their membership is still quite small. But the overall picture is decline, with some women's communities apparently on the way to extinction.

This drop-off has been particularly noticeable in its impact on Catholic schools, where the legendary teaching sisters of the past were at one time a dominant—and revered—presence. Again, numbers tell the story. The 1965 figures for Catholic school teachers were 104,314 nuns and 75,103 laypeople, but since then a dramatic turnaround has taken place, with teaching sisters totaling a meager 4,956 and lay teachers 162,555.

As for the schools themselves, in 1965 there were 10,931 Catholic elementary schools in the United States with 4,566,809 students. Forty-five years later there were 5,990 elementary schools with an enrollment of 1,547,212—an almost two-thirds drop in students. The number of schools and students fell sharply through the 1970s, stabilized for a while, then began falling again. Analysts attribute what has happened at least in part to rising costs associated with replacing low-paid nuns with higher-paid laity. Declines also have occurred on the secondary level, albeit less drastic ones: 1965—2,465 Catholic high schools with 708,708,535 students; 2010—1,338 schools and 647,246 students. (Not surprisingly, the number of pupils enrolled in nonschool religious education programs has gone up over the years, in 2010 reaching 687,174 at the high school level and 3,055,645 at the elementary level.)

Participation in the sacramental life of the Church presents a similarly dismaying picture, with participation in the Eucharist—the Mass—at its heart.

The fashion some years ago, when American Catholic attendance at weekly Mass started to slip, was to say that, after all, going to Mass on Sunday (or Saturday evening, since that option was available by then) wasn't the only, or even the best, test of whether someone was a good Catholic. Not many people say that today, as Mass attendance has continued to fall and the implications of the drop-off—above all, the self-chosen distancing and alienation from the Church that it implies—have sunk in. Plainly there *is* more to being a good Catholic than going to Mass; but people who don't regularly go to Mass can hardly be said to be a meaningful part of the living community of faith that celebrating the Eucharist creates and sustains.

How things stand now on this matter of Mass attendance is more complex, and also more disturbing, than often is recognized. Back in the 1960s, around 70% of American Catholics were at Mass on any given Sunday; now the figure cited varies from source to source, depending on how the data are collected, but one reliable source, the Center for Applied Research in the Apostolate (CARA), reports that 22% of adult American Catholics were weekly Mass attenders in 2010. On a given Sunday, it seems, attendance may rise a bit, perhaps to as much as 30%, because Catholics who drop by for Mass now and then (monthly, at Christmas and Easter, whenever) happen to be in church that week. But now-and-then dropping by, though it may be better than never going to Mass at all, is a far cry from being an engaged member of the Catholic faith community.

Weekly participation in the Sunday Eucharist is the Church's norm for her members. Leaving norms and laws aside, though, wouldn't Catholics who understood and appreciated the Eucharist take weekly participation in Mass to be a minimal, self-imposed standard that they gladly accepted for themselves?

Generational differences are striking here. Among Catholics who grew up before Vatican II, 45% attend Mass weekly or more often, but among younger Catholics, the figure falls as low as 18%. Of course, these figures are much better than the figures for countries like Germany, France, Spain, and Great Britain. In France, for instance, one survey found that from 1972 to 2009 weekly Mass attendance fell from 20% to 4.5%, with more than 65% of 2009's weekly attenders being above the age of 50. But American Catholics can hardly congratulate themselves on their record, considering that by comparison with Eucharistic participation in the not-so-distant past (that 70% weekly Mass attendance rate of the 1960s and earlier), today's figures for the U.S. are dismal.

Reception of the sacrament of penance or reconciliation is in similar straits. As of 2008, according to CARA, 3 out of every 10 American Catholics reported making a sacramental confession less than once a year, with another 45%

saying they never received the sacrament at all. Only 2% reported going to confession monthly or more often. For Catholics who recall the lines of penitents waiting outside confessionals on Saturday nights when they were growing up a half century ago, this is an astonishing change. As with Mass attendance, so also with confession: God can forgive sins in other ways, but it's by no means clear that Catholics who've given up receiving the sacrament of penance, despite its being readily available, have the sorrow for sin and the purpose of amendment that forgiveness of their sins would necessarily require.

The same picture exists in other areas of sacramental participation: Catholic marriages—341,356 in 1990, 267,517 in 2000, and 179,576 in 2010; infant baptisms—1,022,014 in 2000 and 857,410 in 2010; First Communions—884,570 in 2000 and 806,576 in 2010. Down, down, down . . .

The tension that now exists between the teaching of the Church and the attitudes of many American Catholics is illustrated in many of the areas and issues already examined in this book. As this is written, the latest large-scale examination of Catholic attitudes to be published is the fifth Catholics in America study conducted at six-year intervals by a team of social scientists under the direction of William V. D'Antonio. Published in 2011, the latest study found, among much else, that among the 19% of the 1,442 self-identified Catholics whom it surveyed who regard themselves as "highly committed" to the Church, strikingly high percentages believe it is possible to be a good Catholic without attending Mass every Sunday (49%); without following Church doctrine on birth control (60%), divorce and remarriage (46%), and abortion (31%); without being married in the Church (48%); and without giving time or money to help the poor (39%). To the question "who should have the final say" about several moral issues, survey respondents overall chose the answer "individuals" in preference to "church leaders" and "both" by these percentages: divorce and remarriage (47%), abortion (52%), sex outside marriage (53%), homosexuality (57%), and contraception (66%). The survey results, D'Antonio wrote, provide "a portrait showing both persistence and change in the beliefs, practices and attitudes of Catholics".[8]

People looking for reasons to be optimistic about the future of the Church in America sometimes turn to Hispanics and young people. Let's take a quick look at both.

As we've seen, Hispanic immigration and Hispanic birth rates are the main reasons why overall Catholic population in the United States hasn't been dropping for years. As Anglo Catholics exit the Church, Hispanic Catholics arrive, keeping the number of Catholics growing and the Catholic percentage of total U.S. population stable at about 22%. Census figures for 2000 put the number of Hispanics in the country at 35.3 million, with Catholics among them estimated at 73%. About one Catholic in three is Hispanic, with the figure close to half among younger Catholics.

Also on the positive side, Latino Catholics are somewhat more likely not to leave the Church than are non-Latinos. But according to a Pew Forum senior researcher, the difference is not so large as some might expect: "Among non-Hispanics who were raised Catholic, 66 percent are still Catholic; among Hispanics who were raised Catholic, it's

[8] William V. D'Antonio, "Persistence and Change", *National Catholic Reporter*, October 28–November 10, 2011. This issue of the paper contains several articles by D'Antonio and others commenting on the survey along with the survey results themselves.

73 percent. That's a statistically significant difference, but we're not talking about night and day." [9]

Moreover, there are obvious problems within the Latino Catholic community regarding their relationship with the Church. The Catholic News Agency, reporting findings of a Univision and Associated Press poll, cites a "significant gap" between older and younger generations on issues of religion and morality: "The younger generation and those who speak more English than Spanish are less likely to identify as Catholic and are less likely to oppose legalized abortion or gay 'marriage.'" The news agency said the Pew Hispanic Center had confirmed that these findings were "relatively similar" to its findings in a study of Hispanic youth in December 2009. [10]

Does this mean assimilation into American secular culture is having the same impact on Hispanics that it has had in the past on other ethnic groups? And, even if it's somewhat premature to draw that conclusion, should we be surprised if this turns out to be the case? Archbishop José Gomez of Los Angeles, who was born in Monterey, Mexico, and now heads the largest Catholic diocese in the United States, says he believes that "in God's plan, the new Hispanic presence is to advance our country's spiritual renewal." But that will not be so easy. In fact, he holds, the biggest problem facing Hispanic Catholics in the United States is

"the dominant culture ..., which is aggressively, even militantly secularized.... 'Practical atheism' has become the de facto state religion in America. The price of participation in our economic, political, and social life is that we essentially

[9] Allen, "America's Religious Marketplace".
[10] Catholic News Agency, "Poll Finds Catholic Identity of Young Latinos Decreasing", August 11, 2010, http://www.catholicnewsagency.com/news/poll-finds-catholic-identity-of-young-latinos-decreasing/.

have to agree to conduct ourselves as if God does not exist. Religion in the U.S. is something we do on Sundays or in our families, but is not allowed to have any influence on what we do the rest of the week."[11]

Although this is a problem for everyone, not just recently arrived Hispanic Catholics, Archbishop Gomez believes it is especially a problem for them and other immigrant groups. "Immigrants already face severe demands to 'fit in,' to downplay what is culturally and religiously distinct about them; to prove that they are 'real' Americans, too. We might feel subtle pressures to blend in, to assimilate, to downplay our heritage and our distinctive identities as Catholics and Hispanics."

In light of all this, it's reasonable to conclude that preserving the Catholic identity of Latinos in the United States is a touch-and-go proposition now. But the situation is no better, and may be worse, in the case of American Catholic young people.

Certainly there are many high-minded and devout young American Catholics who are strongly committed to their faith. I have met some of them, and I admire them. These are the young people who attend events like World Youth Day, pitch in to make projects in their parishes and schools succeed, sign up for volunteer service programs during vacation or after graduation, participate in Mass and receive the sacraments, strive to live chaste lives despite the influence of the corrupt secular culture surrounding them, marry responsibly with the intention of having Catholic homes and families, or in some cases enter the priesthood and religious life. If the Church in the United States has a future,

[11] Catholic News Agency, "Archbishop Gomez Analyzes Future of Hispanics in US Catholic Church", exclusive interview, May 28, 2010, http://www.catholicnewsagency.com/news/archbishop-gomez-analyzes-future-of-hispanics-in-us-catholic-church/.

these admirable young people are it. But according to the numbers, it's an unpleasant fact that they're a minority even among their Catholic peers, and a small minority at that.[12]

As for American teenagers at large, the massive National Study of Youth and Religion found them to be partial to "Moralistic Therapeutic Deism". The central tenets of this creed include "belief in a God who . . . watches over" people and wants them to be "good, nice and fair", the belief that life's principal goal is "to be happy and to feel good about oneself", and the conviction that there's no need to involve God in one's affairs except to solve one's problems. A writer in a Protestant journal calls this belief system "sinister" inasmuch as for its adherents "it supplants traditional religious faiths."[13]

Even worse from a Catholic point of view, only 10% of Catholic teens reported that religion was "extremely important" to them in shaping their lives. This compares with 20% of mainline Protestant teens, 29% of conservative Protestant teens, and 31% of black Protestant teens. On some measures of religious faith and practice, the Catholics scored lower than some secular Jewish teenagers and those self-identified as "not religious".[14] Replying to a critic who

[12] Writing in a mass-circulation newspaper, a self-identified member of this "strange millennial cohort" attributes its embrace of religious and moral orthodoxy to a sense of having been "betrayed" by "1960s-style liberation". She says: "This tolerant, open-minded ethos seemed to promise freedom: safe-sex with many partners, drugs and alcohol galore and quick, no-fault divorce. So our Baby Boomer parents partied hard, yet in so many cases left us only the hangover: heartbreak, addiction and broken homes, plus rising rates of teenage depression and suicide." Anna Williams, "For These Millennials, Faith Trumps Relativism", *USA Today*, August 17, 2011.

[13] Carol E. Lytch, "What Teens Believe", in *Christian Century*, September 6, 2005 (book review of *Soul Searching: The Religious and Spiritual Lives of American Teenagers*, by Christian Smith, with Melinda Lundquist Denton)

[14] The findings of the National Study of Youth and Religion are reported in Smith, *Soul Searching* and Kenda Creasy Dean, *Almost Christian: What the*

complained that the Catholic teens described in the Catholic chapter of the report weren't typical, the chief researcher for this national study, Christian Smith of the University of North Carolina at Chapel Hill, responded that these young Catholics were "explicitly situated in the overall and clear finding that Catholic teens as a whole are not doing well religiously".

"Of course there are some very solid, committed Catholic teens, but they are not the norm, they are the minority", Smith said.

Forty percent of Catholic teens in the study said they'd never attended any parish-based religious education, compared with 19% of mainline Protestants, 13% of conservative Protestants, and 12% of black Protestants. Predictably, the Catholic teens least attached to the Church usually were the offspring of nonpracticing or semipracticing Catholic parents. "It appears that the relative religious laxity of most U.S. Catholic teenagers significantly reflects the relative religious laxity of their parents", according to Smith.

Since, according to the Pew findings cited above, Catholics who quit the Church commonly take that step in their early twenties, it stands to reason that Catholic retention efforts should be focused on young people before they reach that age. But that's easy to say and not so easy to do. After all, how much opportunity is there for reaching out to Catholic teenagers who live with religiously lax Catholic parents, rarely go to Mass, and don't attend Catholic schools or take part in parish-based religious formation? Offhand, a form of peer ministry would appear to offer very nearly the only realistic hope of doing that. But such peer

---

Faith of Our Teenagers Is Telling the American Church (New York: Oxford University Press, 2010).

ministry hardly exists among American Catholic young people.

So this is the overall picture of American Catholicism today. Of course, it has positive glimmerings here and there: a core of faithful Catholics of all ages—clergy, religious, and laity—deeply committed to the Church, practicing their faith, doing all they can to preach the gospel in the world; a significant number of relatively young Church leaders, bishops and others, who are guiding the Church with courage and pastoral creativity; new candidates for the priesthood and religious life who love the faith and are eager to change things for the better in the face of many obstacles; vibrant dioceses and parishes that have understood what authentic renewal requires and are responding accordingly; and an emerging network of institutions that includes colleges and universities proud to be called Catholic, media-related enterprises, professional organizations, and movements for formation and apostolate. All of the aforementioned are material for the "plausibility structure" of a viable new Catholic subculture.

Yet as matters now stand, the larger picture of American Catholicism is dismal. This is a picture of institutional and human collapse—a startling dropout rate, reflected in the huge number of ex-Catholics in America who've quit the Church and either joined other churches or no church at all; vastly reduced Mass attendance and participation in the sacraments, including penance and matrimony, compared with 50 years ago; the virtual disappearance of twenty-something Catholics from many parishes; widespread rejection of Church teaching, most conspicuous in relation to matters of sexual morality but by no means limited to that; parochial schools shutting their doors for good; colleges and universities that are Catholic in name only (or not even that: "in the Catholic tradition" is an expression now used by many of these institutions to describe their tenuous relationship to the Church); a decline in the number of priests that is rapidly approaching crisis proportions while "no-Mass Sundays" spread in parishes in many parts of the country; aging women's religious congregations headed for extinction; persistent dissent in sectors of the church-related media and a large part of the Catholic theological community; uncertain leaders who appear to be unwilling or unable to provide strong, clear direction yet resist and ridicule those who are less hesitant than themselves; widespread confusion, discouragement, and apathy among Catholic laypeople who still come to church but slog on in a kind of joyless practice of their religion. And much, much more. In the absence of rapid, radical change—and barring a miracle, of course—things can only get worse.

Yet this crisis is still widely ignored by people who ought urgently to be seeking remedies. Some Catholics are simply ignorant of the facts, though perhaps willfully so. That appears to the case with those commentators on Church affairs who apparently are still caught up in the old Americanism and its self-congratulating assessment of Catholic assimilation. They naïvely believe that, in Jay Dolan's words, "at the dawn of the twenty-first century, Catholicism is no longer a stranger in the land. It has found a home in the United States." [15]

Without going quite that far, other Catholics pass their Catholic lives in a state of denial about conditions in the Church. Older Catholics in particular often appear to imagine that little has changed—and certainly nothing for the

---

[15] Jay P. Dolan, *In Search of an American Catholicism: A History of Religion and Culture in Tension* (New York: Oxford University Press, 2002), 11.

worse—since they were growing up in the thriving American Catholicism of the 1940s and 1950s. Denial is their defense. One can imagine them saying, "There's nothing I can do about these problems. Most of them don't touch me directly; I couldn't change them even if they did. So why should I make myself miserable by taking notice of them? Please just leave me in peace."

Sad to say, many Church leaders also close their eyes, at least in public, to the abundant evidence of decline. Perhaps they fear that openly acknowledging the magnitude and seriousness of the crisis would hurt morale and only speed up the collapse. But not everyone considers silence a prudent tactic. Reflecting on the high rate of dropping out from the Church, Peter Steinfels says that more important now from the bishops than a plan of action would be "a sign of determination to address these losses honestly and openly, to absorb the existing data, to gather more if necessary, and to entertain and evaluate a wide range of views about causes and remedies".[16] If the episcopal conference of the United States has been doing that, it's done it—consistent with its established policy of excessive, self-defeating secrecy in the conduct of Church affairs—behind closed doors and without letting people know. (But in fact there's no evidence that it has been done at all, whether secretly or not.)

Steinfels begins his book *A People Adrift* by saying the Catholic Church in America is "on the verge of either an irreversible decline or a thoroughgoing transformation".[17] He's right. But even though Steinfels would prefer a thoroughgoing transformation, his transformational agenda turns

---

[16] Steinfels, "Further Adrift".
[17] Peter Steinfels, *A People Adrift* (New York: Simon and Schuster, 2003), 1.

out to consist of steps that either seem too small to accomplish much or else are highly problematic: "a quantum leap in the quality of Sunday liturgies, including preaching" (excellent idea, but how do you program a quantum leap in the quality of homilies?); "a massive, all-out mobilization" to "catechize the young, bring adolescents into church life, and engage young adults in faith formation" (also excellent, but how do you do it with kids who live with lax Catholic parents who themselves seldom go to church?); "expanding the pool of those eligible for ordination" (ordain women and married men); and "revisiting" Church teaching on sexuality (and see what happened to the Anglican church when it did these things).

Among those who recognize the crisis in American Catholicism for what it is and are deeply troubled by it, one of the few who has attempted seriously to work out the implications of the precipitous and continuing decline documented above is David Carlin. Carlin, a social scientist and former member (Democratic) of the Rhode Island state senate, presented his analysis in a book published in 2003, *The Decline and Fall of the Catholic Church in America*. As the title suggests, it's a sobering study.

The author holds that American Catholicism several decades ago largely abandoned its distinctive identity and became "fully Americanized" after World War II—a *de facto* denominational religion, "on all fours with the Presbyterians, the Methodists, the Episcopalians, et cetera".[18] (This resembles the Protestant-Catholic-Jew pattern of Americanizing the churches that Will Herberg depicted in the 1950s. In those years, this strategy was closely associated

---

[18] David Carlin, *The Decline and Fall of the Catholic Church in America* (Manchester, N.H.: Sophia Institute Press, 2003), 261.

with the dismantling of the Catholic subculture that began around the same time.) In those years it was commonly regarded as a broad-minded, ecumenically sensitive, and eminently American path for the Catholic Church. Many Catholics still see it that way. Unfortunately, it was suicidal. The Episcopal church and the mainline Protestant churches, diminished in numbers and continuing to shrink, have undoubtedly gone farther in this line than the Catholics— they got an earlier start, after all; but in recent decades the Catholics have been hurrying to catch up.

As Carlin sees it, the difficulty with this strategy of ecclesiastical self-destruction is that generically Christian religious bodies have "set their feet on a slippery slope leading to skepticism",[19] with calamitous effects on the faith of their members. The Pew Forum finding that nearly half of all Americans, and nearly one in three who were raised as Catholics, have either changed religion one or more times or dropped out of organized religion entirely, provides support for this observation.

Carlin is scathingly critical of American Catholic leadership during the crucial years immediately after the Second Vatican Council. At a time when leaders were needed of the stature of Washington, Lincoln, and Franklin Roosevelt, he writes, the Church in the United States got "bishops reminding us of James Buchanan and Herbert Hoover". In his estimation, the future is bleak. Although in a "showdown fight for control of American Catholicism" between conservative Catholics and liberal Catholics, the conservatives' "tenacity" makes them likely winners, American Catholicism will by then be "a very poor thing".[20]

---

[19] Ibid., 264.
[20] Ibid., 279.

In sum, it will be forced to retreat to a new Catholic quasi-ghetto. But unlike the old Catholic ghetto—which was optimistic, building up its strength, looking forward to the day when its people would be first-class Americans—this new ghetto will be pessimistic, carrying a memory of failure, realizing that true Catholics will never have an important role to play in what will, by that point, be America's thoroughly secularized dominant culture. This saving remnant will have little or no influence on the larger American society, almost as little as the Amish or the Hasidic Jews have.[21]

I don't cite Carlin because I think he's ineluctably right but because he very well *could* be right, because his prediction is drawn from the analysis of relevant facts like those laid out in this book, and because what he says has been widely ignored by Catholics, including leaders of the Catholic community, who too often appear to be far gone in happy talk and denial. The best way to make certain that Carlin is proved right will of course be to persist in foolish evasion like that.

The problems that now face American Catholicism are serious, numerous, and complex. Moreover, to the extent that they are symptoms of the secularization process under way in many places today, the immediate challenge isn't so much to solve the problems as it is to recognize what is happening and adapt to it in ways faithful to the Catholic tradition but responsive to the needs of rapidly changing times.

---

[21] Ibid., 280. Without sharing this view of the future of American Catholicism, John L. Allen Jr., writing from a liberal Catholic perspective, in effect agrees with Carlin that conservative Catholics—he calls them "evangelical Catholics"—will emerge victorious in the Church in the United States, although the media, because of ideological sympathy, will continue to focus largely on liberal Catholicism. See John L. Allen Jr., *The Future Church* (New York: Doubleday, 2009), 54–94.

Still, certain remedial steps can and should be taken. Taking them won't be easy, but at least it will be a move in the right direction for American Catholics to agree on what these steps are. I list my preferences sequentially, but I'm aware that they are interlocking and that efforts to accomplish them all must take place simultaneously.

First, then, it is necessary to restore—or, more properly, create—a healthy Catholic subculture in America. The old Catholic subculture, with all its strengths and limitations, was the bedrock foundation of American Catholicism until well into the twentieth century. Then, weakened by demographic shifts and cultural revolution, it was tossed aside by Catholic intellectuals and the leaders of the Church. There is no bringing it back to life now, as some Catholic nostalgia buffs apparently would like to have happen. But the need is imperative for a new subculture and its supporting plausibility structure as the underpinning for American Catholicism in the twenty-first century.

When I speak of creating a new Catholic subculture, the reaction often is, "That isn't realistic. What you're talking about can't be done." But it's the skepticism that is unrealistic, for that supposedly undoable project is, for better or for worse, already taking shape—right before the skeptics' eyes, if they would only open them and see.

To be sure, a viable culture or subculture has to arise spontaneously, organically as it were, from the lived experience of people sharing common values and aspirations. From this point of view, the idea of creating a culture undoubtedly is unrealistic. But it is not unrealistic at all to think of creating the institutional embodiments of a plausibility structure that will express and foster the shared values of people who are already sympathetic to the enterprise. This is what the Catholic Church in the United States should be doing now. If successful, the structure will become the framework of a new Catholic subculture.

As suggested, furthermore, to some extent it's already happening, partly in response to the challenge of preserving—and in a number of cases re-Catholicizing—older Catholic institutions that could have roles to play in a new Catholic subculture if, but *only* if, they return to the strong, clear Catholic identity they had in the past. Many American Catholic colleges and universities are illustrations of this. Increasingly too this need exists in relation to Catholic social services (Catholic Charities, Catholic Relief Services, acute care Catholic hospitals) where the lure of government money and growing secularist pressure to conform combine to threaten their identity as authentically Catholic programs. Says Archbishop Charles Chaput:

> "Catholic ministries have the duty to faithfully embody Catholic beliefs on marriage, the family, social justice, sexuality, abortion and other important issues. And if the state refuses to allow those Catholic ministries to be faithful in their services through legal or financial bullying, then as a matter of integrity they should end their services." [22]

To which one might add that if that in fact is the way this growing church-state struggle turns out, it could trigger a turn to the kind of personalized, deinstitutionalized charity urged on a number of occasions by Pope Benedict XVI and Blessed John Paul II, which in turn would be a significant contribution to building up the new Catholic subculture of the future.

---

[22] Charles J. Chaput, O.F.M.Cap., "Catholic Identity and the Future of Catholic Social Ministry", *Origins*, August 4, 2011.

To repeat: The new Catholic subculture is not a pipe dream. Already it is taking shape here and there. Many times it represents a reaction by individuals and families against what they rightly perceive as a morally destructive American secular culture. Some homeschool their children. Others have given up on television and carefully police access to the Internet in their homes. Still others have taken the radical step of moving out of big cities and their suburbs to smaller, quieter, more conservative, and less culturally threatening communities where the assaults on their eyes, ears, and morals—and those of their children—are less flagrant.

Signs of an emerging Catholic subculture also include institutional embodiments proper to a plausibility structure: proudly orthodox new Catholic colleges and universities (and a few that are not new but have taken serious steps to refurbish their Catholic identity); new, similarly orthodox religious communities; media ventures like EWTN and Catholic radio, along with a growing number of websites and some periodicals and publishing houses; professional organizations (e.g., the Fellowship of Catholic Scholars, the Society of Catholic Social Scientists) and some old-line general membership groups (e.g., the Knights of Columbus, which remains by far the largest Catholic organization in America); and groups and movements committed to promoting an authentically Catholic spirituality for laywomen and laymen living and working in the secular world. Side by side with these are individual parishes and even whole dioceses that have taken this same message to heart. Highly encouraging too is the appearance on the scene of a new generation of bishops and priests, traditional minded but fully up-to-date in style, who take a realistic view of the present situation of American Catholicism and are responding realistically to it.

The Church in the United States has far to go to create a new subculture comparable to the one that was so recklessly abandoned in the 1960s and 1970s. And some manifestations of the new subculture have troubling characteristics, including being too cozy with the political and cultural Far Right, where libertarian attitudes and principles opposed to those of the Catholic Church sometimes predominate. To be integrally Catholic, the new subculture must be not only pro-life—though it must certainly be that—but active on the broad range of issues embraced by the social doctrine of the Church as it's been developed by the papal Magisterium since the days of Leo XIII. Subsidiarity, socialization, and solidarity *all* play central roles in this body of teaching. Needless to say too, the new subculture must be open to a variety of sometimes conflicting prudential judgments about how best to realize good purposes in concrete political and social circumstances. In the end, the Church must resist being co-opted by any political party or political agenda, left or right, precisely in order to remain an unencumbered critic of them all.

The new subculture will need to take fully and creatively into account the rapidly growing Hispanic presence in American Catholicism. The 2010 census counted more than 50 million Hispanics—about one in every six Americans—who accounted for over half the country's growth from 2000 to 2010. Nearly three out of four of them are Catholics. In recent decades, the Church in America has made serious efforts to accommodate and integrate this growing body of Latinos in her ranks, and these efforts must continue and expand. It would be tragic if the new subculture turned out to be the preserve of aging Catholic Anglos.

Unlike the old Catholic subculture, the new subculture must be one in which clericalism and the abuse of secrecy are no longer taken for granted but instead are actively resisted. The problem of clericalism has already been discussed in relation to the scandal of clergy sex abuse. Here something needs to be said about the abuse of secrecy, which in ecclesiastical contexts serves as clericalism's accomplice and enabler.

It would be absurd to suppose that the abuse of secrecy is peculiar to the Catholic Church. It's found in government, the military, academia, the private sector, and even in the media—wherever those in charge resort to concealment to cover up mistakes or control the people under them or just because they find secrecy more convenient than openness and accountability. In the Church, however, the clergy are the people in charge, the management class, which is why secrecy in the Church so readily becomes a tool of the clericalist culture: this is how clericalism works.

Elsewhere I've argued at length that the systematic abuse of secrecy contradicts the Church's nature as *communio*[23]—a communion or hierarchically structured community of faith within which all members are fundamentally equal in dignity and rights.[24] But equality in dignity and rights aren't truly present in a community in which a significant body of members are routinely denied information that they need

[23] See Russell Shaw, *Nothing to Hide: Secrecy, Communication and Community in the Catholic Church* (San Francisco: Ignatius Press, 2008).

[24] Vatican Council II, Dogmatic Constitution on the Church, *Lumen gentium*, no. 32: "[T]here is a common dignity of members deriving from their rebirth in Christ, a common grace as sons, a common vocation to perfection, one salvation, one hope and undivided charity. In Christ and in the Church there is, then, no inequality arising from race or nationality, social condition or sex.... Although by Christ's will some are established as teachers, dispensers of the mysteries and pastors for the others, there remains, nevertheless, a true equality between all with regard to the dignity and to the activity which is common to all the faithful in the building up of the Body of Christ." Cf. canon 208 of the *Code of Canon Law*.

in order to function as full, equal members.[25] The abuse of secrecy therefore must not be given a home in the new Catholic subculture.

Although the primary purpose of the subculture and its plausibility structure should be to preserve, foster, and transmit the Catholic identity of Catholics, it's crucially important that they not become inward-looking, merely defensive instruments for shielding people on the inside from what lies outside—a ghetto, that's to say—as David Carlin suggests may happen. It's no idle concern. John Allen describes the early years of the twenty-first century as "a boom time for the fortress mentality in Catholicism, especially at the leadership level". He adds:

> "Church/state clashes over abortion and homosexuality, coupled with perceptions that the church has become a scapegoat for a much broader social problem with sexual abuse, have fueled an increasingly defensive psychology. Many church leaders have become more prone to interpret disagreement as defiance, more cautious about contamination by secular values, and less inclined to explain themselves to people they believe don't really want to understand." [26]

Not all of these reactions are entirely bad, and many of the perceptions that give rise to them are correct. "Contamination by secular values", as Allen calls it, is a very real

[25] Sissela Bok notes the paradoxical character of secrecy: "Secret practices protect the liberty of some while impairing that of others. They guard intimacy and creativity, yet tend to spread and to invite abuse. Secrecy can enhance a sense of brotherhood, loyalty, and equality among insiders while kindling discrimination against outsiders." Sissela Bok, *Secrets: On the Ethics of Concealment and Revelation* (New York: Vintage Books, 1983), xvi.

[26] John L. Allen Jr., "Crucifix Case a Victory for 'Open Door' Catholicism", All Things Catholic, *National Catholic Reporter*, March 24, 2011, http://ncronline.org/blogs/all-things-catholic/crucifix-case-victory-open-door-catholicism.

problem, and action by the Church is necessary to preserve her members from it to the extent possible. But the defensive and reactionary posture to which this can give rise has troubling implications for the American Catholicism of the future.

Francis Cardinal George sums up the overall situation with admirable clarity:

> [W]e have to recognize what we are up against. The world is both friendly and unfriendly, both holy and demonic. The world will welcome some of our criticisms and will do everything it can to contest others. When we hear the demands of the world, which we have to hear, lest we fail to attend to the signs of the times, the great missionary challenge then is to discern what the Church must adapt to and what is incompatible with the faith.[27]

Against this background, it should be clear why the assimilation of American Catholics into a secular culture shaped by the Rawlsian understanding of liberal democracy is such a troubling development.[28] J. Brian Benestad, in his comprehensive analysis of Catholic social doctrine *Church, State, and Society*, cites Princeton politics professor Stephen Macedo's cheerful claim that the experience of cultural assimilation has transformed American Catholicism into "a positive and in many instances decisive force for the liberalization" of Catholicism elsewhere.[29] This of course is by no means

[27] Francis George, O.M.I., *The Difference God Makes: A Catholic Vision of Faith, Communion, and Culture* (New York: Crossroad, 2009), 181.

[28] John Rawls (1921–2002) was an influential American philosopher in the liberal tradition who in works like *A Theory of Justice* (1971) and *Political Liberalism* (1993) laid out a political philosophy organized around justice as fairness and based upon what critics describe as an implicit moral relativism.

[29] Stephen Macedo, quoted in J. Brian Benestad, *Church, State, and Society: An Introduction to Catholic Social Doctrine* (Washington, D.C.: Catholic University of America Press, 2011), 435.

entirely bad, but at its deepest level this state of affairs unavoidably raises the question: What *is* this culture of Rawlsian liberal democracy into which American Catholics have been assimilated and that they now are helping spread to the Church in other countries? Benestad describes it like this:

> "In sum, liberalism tends to promote individualism, the separation of rights from duties, the loosening of commitments in families and at work, undue sympathy for the principle of autonomy and 'the culture of death,' more deference to reigning opinions than to Church authority, the reception of revealed religion as opinion, and understanding morality more in terms of rights and values than virtues." [30]

Here is a world view that the new Catholic subculture must reject for itself while also working actively to convert those who hold it.

This evangelistic emphasis must be consistently expressed in the institutions and programs of the Catholic plausibility structure as a part of the Church's overall program of new evangelization. Nonpracticing and seldom-practicing Catholics should be among the objects of this new evangelization, not excluded from the embrace of the subculture or treated with scorn (or, for that matter, as today often happens, viewed unrealistically as other than what they truly are—Catholics with dangerously tenuous ties to the faith—and treated just as if they were solid Catholics in good standing just like those who practice their faith).

There is an obvious potential tension here, between the emphasis on preserving and transmitting Catholic identity and the emphasis on evangelizing culture. With a modicum

---

[30] Ibid., 336. A friend of mine adds that most of today's liberal Catholic moral discourse is accurately described as "soft dissent".

of self-awareness and creativity on the part of faithful Catholics, however, the tension needn't degenerate into conflict and can in fact supply helpful intellectual and spiritual energy in both spheres.

The subculture must also take a fresh, creative look at the role of the laity. The greatest failure of the post–Vatican II Church, Cardinal George says, has been a failure

> "to call forth and form a laity engaged in the world politically, economically, culturally, and socially, on faith's terms rather than on the world's terms. If perhaps we paid less attention to ministries and to expertise and to functions, necessary though all of that is, and more to mission or purpose, then we might recapture the sense of what should be genuinely new as a result of the Council."[31]

Catholic laypeople must be the new subculture's primary agents of evangelization. If they aren't, then it is certain that no one else will step up to take their place, and Carlin's bleak vision will be on the way to becoming reality. Here, perhaps more than anywhere else, the reality of personal vocation (discussed below) comes into play.

In the United States as in other Western countries, militant secularism's campaign against organized religion is growing in force and boldness. No longer do secularists simply seek to win legalization and social approval for abortion, same-sex marriage, and other familiar items on their to-do list. They do seek such approval, certainly, but more to the point, their long-range goal can be seen to be the disabling of religion and its removal as a significant cultural agent. In this they have been increasingly successful since

[31] George, *Difference*, 180.

the middle years of the last century, driving mainline Protestantism from the field three or four decades ago so that little except the Catholic Church, evangelical Protestants, and the Mormons stand in opposition in our continuing culture war.[32]

The secularist campaign has taken a somewhat different tack. Years ago the Church fought to prevent bad things from happening—things like family planning as an instrument of government policy, permissive abortion laws, gay rights measures conferring entitlements on homosexual unions. Often, of course, the Church's resistance to such things was inconsistent and not very effective; often she lost. The continuing campaign begun in 2011 by the American bishops to defend and promote the principle of religious liberty in the United States is a belated and badly needed effort in this line whose results cannot be predicted.

But *The Cardinal* tells a different story. That fictional mirror of the Catholic psyche at midpoint in the twentieth century contains an episode in which Stephen Fermoyle bests a supercilious society woman who is pushing Planned Parenthood as the way of keeping lower-class breeding under control. Fermoyle is widely admired for his triumph. But this is a novel, after all, and the incident is set in the 1930s. Fermoyle and his era are no more today. Now Planned Parenthood and its powerful friends are largely calling the shots.

The big change began with policies that were part of Lyndon Johnson's War on Poverty; these policies were reinforced and expanded under Richard Nixon. The American bishops raised few objections to making the promotion of birth control for the poor a matter of government

---

[32] See Ross Douthat, *Bad Religion: How We Became a Nation of Heretics* (New York: Free Press, 2012), 83–112.

policy and merely asked that the government not be coercive.[33] And today, as suggested, the Church's struggle with the secularist foe has entered a new, more sinister phase in which the Church finds herself having to resist government initiatives that force the Church to cooperate in various forms of officially sponsored immorality—for example, by using antidiscrimination laws to force Church-sponsored adoption agencies to accept gay couples as adoptive parents or go out of business. This trend reached new heights in 2011 with a mandate issued by the U.S. Department of Health and Human Services requiring Catholic and other religiously affiliated colleges and universities, charities, and hospitals to provide coverage for contraception, abortifacient drugs, and sterilization under their employee health plans.

As of fall 2012, the battle over the mandate was still under way, with the outcome very much in doubt. But already this instance of government overreaching contrary to the First Amendment's free exercise clause has had at least one surprisingly positive result. Instead of complying with the mandate or closing the institutions affected, the American bishops, as noted above, launched a counterattack intended to meet not only this threat but similar threats to religious liberty from secularist sources.

This will be a long, hard struggle. What can be said with certainty, though, is that many American Catholics responded enthusiastically to the bishops' initiative, saying in effect, "High time we fought back!" There is much encouragement in the readiness of loyal Catholics to enter into this struggle to defend and preserve the interests of their Church.

---

[33] See Donald T. Critchlow, *Intended Consequences: Birth Control, Abortion, and the Federal Government in Modern America* (New York: Oxford University Press, 1999), 50–111.

Not only that—Catholic resistance to militant secularism could in fact be the best kind of evangelization available to the Church today, the most effective form of "new evangelization" available in these troubled times. Recent converts to Catholicism not infrequently report that they were repelled by the growing depravity of the secular culture and attracted to Catholicism as virtually the only serious response to it.

Not long ago I spent an evening with Catholic friends enjoying conversation and good food. One of the group was a highly intelligent man who not long before had entered the Church, and somebody asked him why. This is what he said:

"I'd reached a point in my life when I found myself puzzling over the big questions—the meaning of it all and what I was doing here and where I was going. That kind of thing.

"After a while, I came to a conclusion. There are two and only two real options—atheism and Catholicism. The other possibilities just aren't in the running; they can't compete. So I thought it over, and I decided that Catholicism was the better bet.

"And that's why I became a Catholic."

Not everyone will get to the point in his life where the options become so clear, and not all those who do get to that point will reach the same conclusion. But it's reasonable to suppose that more will find themselves traveling the same intellectual and spiritual path as the options continue to narrow and increasingly stand out in stark relief in the face of militant secularism's relentless cultural imperialism. As this happens, these people will turn to the Catholic Church or recommit themselves to the Church they'd earlier abandoned. They will be welcome reinforcements in an escalating culture war in which the persecution of religion will also be the occasion for a new evangelization of America.

The future of Catholicism in the United States is bound to be painful and hard, just as Orestes Brownson realized many years ago, but it may also prove to be as exciting and ennobling as Brownson's friend and opponent Isaac Hecker hoped. Yet even if Catholic Christianity does emerge victorious in America in the end, its victory will not come about by the means secular culture favors—manipulation, propaganda, coercion—but in the manner peculiar to Christ's Church from the very beginning.

On this matter too the Gibbons Legacy has something to say to us.

In 1876 James Gibbons published a little book of popular apologetics called *The Faith of Our Fathers*. It quickly became a phenomenal success as a tool of apologetics, evangelization, and convert making, and remains in print even now. According to Gibbons' biographer, it is "among the most widely read books on religion in the English language".[34]

The contents and form of *The Faith of Our Fathers* were shaped during the future cardinal's years as vicar apostolic of North Carolina (1868–1872) and bishop of Richmond (1872–1877) while traveling about his far-flung territory preaching and speaking to his scattered Catholic flock and sometimes even to non-Catholic audiences. John Tracy Ellis remarks that Gibbons "gleaned a wealth of experience and knowledge of the non-Catholic mentality from these visits through rural Virginia and North Carolina and it was this enrichment of mind that gave to his first and most famous

[34] John Tracy Ellis, *The Life of James Cardinal Gibbons, Archbishop of Baltimore, 1834–1921* (Milwaukee: Bruce, 1952), 1:151.

book ... an approach and a tone which rapidly made it the *vade mecum* of so many non-Catholic Americans".[35]

In the introduction, the author speaks with feeling about his intentions in writing. As you read his words, it's easy to imagine this young bishop's troubling encounters with Protestant suspicion of and hostility toward Catholics as he found it in rural areas of two southern states nearly a century and a half ago. "Had I been educated as they were, and surrounded by an atmosphere hostile to the Church," he concedes, "perhaps I should be unfortunate enough to be breathing vengeance against her today, instead of consecrating my life to her defence."[36] Now he aims to educate and convince these people regarding the truth and beauty of Catholicism. "This, friendly reader, is my only motive. I feel in the depth of my heart that, in possessing Catholic faith, I hold a treasure compared with which all things earthly are but dross. Instead of wishing to bury this treasure in my breast, I long to share it with you, especially as I lose no part of my spiritual riches by communicating them to you."[37] And he uses a homely metaphor to offer reassurance to that "friendly reader": "In coming to the Church, you are not entering a strange place, but you are returning to your Father's home. The house and furniture may look odd to you, but it is just the same as your forefathers left it three hundred years ago."[38]

Today, of course, we wouldn't make our appeal—not just to Protestants but also to the unchurched and to

[35] Ibid., 145.

[36] James Gibbons, *The Faith of Our Fathers: Being a Plain Exposition and Vindication of the Church Founded by Our Lord Jesus Christ* (1876; facsimile ed., Amsterdam: Fredonia Books, 2004), xiii.

[37] Ibid., xiv.

[38] Ibid., xv.

nonpracticing and semipracticing Catholics—in the language of Victorian-era piety. But in order to evangelize—or, more properly, reevangelize—the spiritual wasteland of secular America, the people of the new Catholic subculture will need the same faith-filled spirit that Gibbons manifested. Lacking that, they will surely not succeed.

As that suggests, the key to new evangelization as a high priority of a new American Catholic subculture isn't institutions and programs. They are important, of course, but they will accomplish very little unless they arise from and express something else—new attitudes: new ways of looking at the Church, the world, and the relationship of American Catholics to both. Even more than material resources, we need an infusion of new thinking and new spirit.

Where, though, are clericalized and sometimes dispirited people—which is what many American Catholics now are—supposed to acquire these things? There's no mystery about that. Indispensable to and inseparable from what's envisaged here is a great deepening of the interior life, the life of the spirit, among American Catholics. It must begin with the believing, practicing Catholics who now make up the shrinking backbone of American Catholicism but who've grown weary, perhaps discouraged, in the face of setbacks, disappointments, and defeats since the 1960s—to say nothing of the alarming custom of rewarding dissenters and dissent practiced by some bishops and religious superiors and heads of Church institutions during much of this time.

A wise friend of mine with whom I was discussing these matters said, "The biggest problem of all—and the cause of all the rest—is that we haven't preached holiness." Fairness, kindness, goodness, tolerance, helping out in the parish, giving to the latest disaster relief campaign—the litany of attractive middle-class virtues and their associated behaviors has indeed been preached and practiced in Catholic America, as has the desirability of getting active in some kind of "ministry" in the parish. But the stern ascesis of abandonment into the hands of a God whose love is a living flame? You must be kidding.

So where to begin? It has to start with the idea of vocation: with preaching and teaching and writing and broadcasting in every available forum the message that God intends each of us to play a unique, unrepeatable role in his providential redemptive plan. Every life, as several recent popes have remarked, is a vocation. The common Catholic assumption that the word "vocation" refers only to a calling to a state in life, and that among the limited possibilities, callings to the clerical and religious states are the only real, authentic vocations that count, is a destructive fallacy typical of the clericalist mentality still commonly shared by priests and Catholic laypeople alike.

Today it is not merely desirable but imperative that Catholics acknowledge the reality of unique personal vocation as preached and taught by such figures as Saint Francis de Sales, Blessed John Henry Newman, and Blessed John Paul II and, having acknowledged this reality, that they get on with the work of discerning, accepting, and living out their own personal vocations—the particular roles God means for them to play in the great work of redemption.[39] "The fundamental objective of the formation of the lay faithful", says John Paul II, "is an ever-clearer discovery of one's vocation and the ever-greater willingness to live it so as to fulfill one's mission. . . . This personal vocation and mission defines

[39] For a treatment of personal vocation that examines the history and theology of the idea along with the practice of vocational discernment, see Germain Grisez and Russell Shaw, *Personal Vocation: God Calls Everyone by Name* (Huntington, Ind.: Our Sunday Visitor Publishing Division, 2003).

the dignity and the responsibility of each member of the lay faithful and makes up the focal point of the whole work of formation." [40]

At this point I turn to the words of a woman who several years ago took a course I taught on the Catholic laity and their place in the Church. She later e-mailed me to share an experience she'd had.

"Last week I gave a lecture to a group of women, and as an opening exercise I asked them to write on one side of the page all the everyday things they do in the course of a day or so. Then I asked them to write on the other side all the things they do in the same time frame that they consider to be holy.

"Without exception, they made up two entirely different lists—on the one hand, daily chores and activities, and on the other hand things associated with what they consider to be 'ministry'—serving as minister of Communion or lector, attending Mass, things like that.

"Many had only one or two items in that second column. No one simply drew an arrow from the daily activities to the list of 'holy' things.

"My lecture was about the apostolate of the laity. If nothing else, I wanted the women to come away from it with a sense of the dignity of our mission as laypeople. That includes understanding that everyday activities really are holy when we do them as faithful Christians and that in this context we aren't called only to *receive* the sacraments but, in a sense, to *be* sacrament and to live sacramental lives in which Christ's presence can be seen. . . .

[40] Post-Synodal Apostolic Exhortation on the Vocation and the Mission of the Lay Faithful in the Church and in the World, *Christifideles laici* (1989), no. 58, in *The Post-Synodal Apostolic Exhortations of John Paul II*, ed. J. Michael Miller, C.S.B. (Huntington, Ind.: Our Sunday Visitor, 1998), 450.

"When the women took a second look at their lists and reflected on their everyday work as a vehicle for spreading the gospel and acting as Christ's missionaries and apostles, they began to personalize what apostolate meant for them."

While this by itself might not serve as the blueprint for a program of new evangelization, it does make clear the indispensable point where any such program must begin—in a well-developed understanding of personal vocation made operative in the lives of all Catholics (or at least in the lives of as many as are able and willing to understand and accept it). Not so coincidentally, a proper understanding of personal vocation is also the indispensable foundation of the spiritual renewal of American Catholicism within the institutional and programmatic structures of a new subculture.

The value and meaning laypeople attach to their everyday lives in the secular world are crucial to discerning their personal vocations as well as to their understanding of their role in the mission of the Church. At the moment, this is an area where confusion reigns—as it has for a long, long time. The novelist and short story writer Flannery O'Connor got to the heart of it years ago. Someone had asked the author of *Wise Blood* and *The Violent Bear It Away*, powerful tales of Bible Belt prophets in radical conflict with a de-Christianized world, why she, a Catholic, wrote about Protestants instead of her fellow Catholics. This in part was her reply:

> To a lot of Protestants I know, monks and nuns are fanatics, none greater. And to a lot of the monks and nuns I know, my Protestant prophets are fanatics. For my part, I think the only difference between them is that if you are a Catholic and have this intensity of belief you join the convent and are heard from no more; whereas if you are a Protestant and have it, there is no convent for you to join and

you go about in the world, getting into all sorts of trouble
and drawing the wrath of people who don't believe anything much at all down on your head.[41]

This was a very shrewd remark, delineating with accuracy as
well as humor the clericalist idea of vocation that she found
among her clericalized fellow Catholics: "[I]f you are a Catholic and have ... intensity of belief you join a convent." Not
much encouragement there for laypeople living in the world.
Alongside the temptation to co-optation by the secular to
which many American Catholics today have succumbed is a
second age-old temptation against healthy Catholic engagement with the world: excessive other-worldliness, or the temptation to spurn the world and withdraw from it as much as
possible. The Second Vatican Council pointed to a very different solution: to build up the kingdom by working here
and now for the realization of human goods.

[I]t is here that the body of a new human family grows,
foreshadowing in some way the age which is to come....
When we have spread on earth the fruits of our nature and
our enterprise—human dignity, brotherly communion, and
freedom—according to the command of the Lord and in
his Spirit, we will find them once again, illuminated and
transfigured, when Christ presents to his Father an eternal
and universal kingdom "of truth and life, a kingdom of
holiness and grace, a kingdom of justice, love and peace"
(preface for the Feast of Christ the King). Here on earth
the kingdom is mysteriously present; when the Lord comes
it will enter into its perfection.[42]

[41] Letter to Sister Mariella Gable, May 4, 1963, in *Flannery O'Connor:
Collected Works*, ed. Sally Fitzgerald (New York: Library of America, 1988),
1183.

[42] Vatican Council II, Pastoral Constitution on the Church in the Modern World, *Gaudium et spes*, no. 39.

It is imperative that American Catholic laypeople—not only for their own sakes but for the sake of the Church and society—discern and accept their personal vocations, fully understanding them to be rooted in and directed to the secular order perceived in this way. The renewal of American Catholicism that is now so urgently needed rests ultimately with them.

There is, however, another, indispensable element that also belongs to the Gibbons Legacy. *The Faith of Our Fathers* makes that clear: "We are commanded by Jesus, suffering and dying for us, to imitate Him by the crucifixion of our flesh, and by acts of daily mortification. 'If anyone,' He says, 'will come after Me, let him deny himself, and take up his cross daily and follow Me.' " [43]

Eat of the fruit, the serpent coaxed Eve, "and you will be like God" (Gen 3:5). Acting at the encouragement of a seductive secularized culture, American Catholics for a long time have gorged themselves on its fruit while their godliness declined.

An insightful friend of mine declares "taking heaven for granted and being afraid of mentioning hell" to be "at the center of what is wrong with the Church". Is that judgment too harsh? During an academic symposium on new evangelization held in late 2011, one speaker, asked how to communicate with the "everyday Catholic", replied, "The first thing is preaching, the second thing is preaching, and the third thing is preaching"; in most Catholic parishes today, he added, the homilies are "abysmal". But a woman who teaches moral theology asked how it is possible to preach to a typical congregation that includes among its

[43] Gibbons, *Faith of Our Fathers*, 2.

members habitual fornicators, men addicted to pornography, and women who've lately had abortions—often, at the urging of husbands or boyfriends—while most people don't even care to hear the words "sin" and "hell" spoken with serious intent. No one hazarded an answer to her question.

Against this background, Pope Benedict insists that the way of the cross is an appropriate, even necessary, way of life, not only for individual Catholics but for the Church herself. Quoting Saint Paul—"God chose what is weak in the world to shame the strong" (1 Cor 1:27)—he says it is "for this reason" that "the Church has no fear of poverty, contempt or persecution in a society which is often attracted by material well-being and worldly power." [44]

However, rather than ending with pious rhetoric in the Victorian manner, with the painful example of our first parents, or with a papal exhortation to a group of pilgrims, I prefer to draw these reflections on the Americanization of American Catholics to a close on a thoroughly American Catholic note.

J. F. Powers was not a prolific writer, but he was a subtle and gifted one, with a knack for skewering the foibles of fellow Catholics whose lifestyle had other sources than *The Imitation of Christ*. In his short story *Prince of Darkness*, an archbishop says of the gaggle of sinners and less-than-saints who were then calling themselves the Body of Christ and would soon take cheerfully to calling themselves the People of God: "We square the circle beautifully. . . . We bring neither peace nor a sword. The rich give us money. We give them consolation and make the eye of the needle a gate.

Together we try to reduce the Church, the Bride of Christ, to a streetwalker." [45]

In his second, and last, novel *Wheat That Springeth Green*, published in 1988, Powers writes about a priest named Joe. In his seminary days he'd experimented with wearing a hair shirt, but now he finds life in his post–Vatican II parish to be all the hair shirt he can handle and then some. In a gesture reminiscent of an incident in the life of Saint John Vianney, patron saint of parish priests, Joe deserts his post and runs away. But, also like the Curé of Ars, he relents and turns back.

Soon after, friends throw a birthday party for Joe. After it's over, he's heading to his car when another priest calls after him about a chair that he's offered to give Joe and that Joe has declined. These are the last words of the novel:

"'*Sure* you don't want that *chair?*'

"Joe shook his head and kept going, calling back, '*Yes,*' and when Dave called after him, 'Where is it you're stationed now—Holy ... Faith?' Joe shook his head and kept going, calling back, '*Cross.*'" [46]

The Catholic Church in America today is stationed at Holy Cross. We can try to run away or we can do our best to embrace the way of the Lord Jesus, which, here and now and always, is the way of the cross. There is no third option.

---

[45] J. F. Powers, "Prince of Darkness", in *Prince of Darkness, and Other Stories* (Garden City, N.Y.: Image Books, 1958), 192.

[46] J. F. Powers, *Wheat That Springeth Green* (New York: Alfred A. Knopf, 1988), 335.

SOURCES CONSULTED

Sources consulted in writing *The Gibbons Legacy* include the following.

Abbott, Walter M., S.J., ed. "Pope John's Opening Speech to the Council". In *The Documents of Vatican II*. New York: American Press, 1966.

Alberigo, Giuseppe. *A Brief History of Vatican II*. Maryknoll, N.Y.: Orbis Books, 2006.

Allen, John L., Jr. *The Future Church*. New York: Doubleday, 2009.

Appleby, R. Scott. *"Church and Age Unite!": The Modernist Impulse in American Catholicism*. Notre Dame, Ind.: University of Notre Dame Press, 1992.

Benestad, J. Brian. *Church, State, and Society: An Introduction to Catholic Social Doctrine*. Washington, D.C.: Catholic University of America Press, 2011.

Berger, Peter L. *A Rumor of Angels: Modern Society and the Rediscovery of the Supernatural*. Garden City, N.Y.: Anchor Books, 1970.

Bok, Sissela. *Secrets: On the Ethics of Concealment and Revelation*. New York: Vintage Books, 1983.

Cafardi, Nicholas P. *Before Dallas: The U.S. Bishops' Response to Clergy Sexual Abuse of Children*. Mahwah, N.J.: Paulist Press, 2008.

Carey, Patrick W. *Orestes A. Brownson: American Religious Weathervane*. Grand Rapids, Mich.: William B. Eerdmans, 2004.

Carlin, David. *The Decline and Fall of the Catholic Church in America*. Manchester, N.H.: Sophia Institute Press, 2003.

The Causes and Context of Sexual Abuse of Minors by Catholic Priests in the United States, 1950–2010: A Report Presented to the United States Conference of Catholic Bishops by the John Jay College Research Team. Washington, D.C.: United States Conference of Catholic Bishops, 2011.

Chaput, Charles, J., O.F.M.Cap. "Catholic Identity and the Future of Catholic Social Ministry". *Origins*, August 4, 2011.

Chinnici, Joseph P., O.F.M. *Living Stones: The History and Structure of Catholic Spiritual Life in the United States*. New York: Macmillan, 1989.

Critchlow, Donald T. *Intended Consequences: Birth Control, Abortion, and the Federal Government in Modern America*. New York: Oxford University Press, 1999.

D'Antonio, William V., James D. Davidson, Dean R. Hoge, and Mary L. Gautier. *American Catholics Today: New Realities of Their Faith and Their Church*. Lanham, Md.: Rowman and Littlefield, 2007.

Day, Dorothy. *The Long Loneliness: The Autobiography of Dorothy Day*. Garden City, N.Y.: Image Books, 1959.

Dean, Kenda Creasy. *Almost Christian: What the Faith of Our Teenagers Is Telling the American Church*. New York: Oxford University Press, 2010.

Dolan, Jay P. *In Search of an American Catholicism: A History of Religion and Culture in Tension*. New York: Oxford University Press, 2002.

Douthat, Ross. *Bad Religion: How We Became a Nation of Heretics*. New York: Free Press, 2012.

Ellis, John Tracy. *American Catholicism*. Rev. 2nd ed. Chicago: University of Chicago Press, 1969.

———. *American Catholics and the Intellectual Life*. Chicago: Heritage Foundation, 1956.

———, ed. *Documents of American Catholic History*. Milwaukee: Bruce, 1962.

———. *The Life of James Cardinal Gibbons, Archbishop of Baltimore, 1834–1921*. 2 vols. Milwaukee: Bruce, 1952.

Farrell, James T. *The Young Manhood of Studs Lonigan*. In *Studs Lonigan*. New York: Signet Books, 1958.

Faulhaber, Michael. "The Essential Characteristics of Catholic Action". In *Readings for Catholic Action*, edited by Burton Confrey. Manchester, N.H.: Magnificat Press, 1937.

Fichter, Joseph H., S.J. "The Americanization of Catholicism". In *Roman Catholicism and the American Way of Life*, edited by Thomas T. McAvoy, CSC., 113–27. Notre Dame, Ind.: University of Notre Dame Press, 1960.

Flannery, Austin, O.P., ed. *Vatican Council II: The Conciliar and Post Conciliar Documents*. Northport, N.Y.: Costello.

Fogarty, Gerald P., S.J. "Francis J. Spellman: American and Roman". In *Patterns of Episcopal Leadership*, 216–34. New York: Macmillan, 1989.

———. *The Vatican and the Americanist Crisis: Denis J. O'Connell, American Agent in Rome, 1885–1903*. Rome: Università Gregoriana Editrice, 1974.

George, Francis, O.M.I. *The Difference God Makes: A Catholic Vision of Faith, Communion, and Culture*. New York: Crossroad, 2009.

Gibbons, James. "The Apostolic Mission of the Irish Race". In *A Retrospect of Fifty Years*, 2:170–89. Baltimore: John Murphy, 1916.

———. *The Faith of Our Fathers: Being a Plain Exposition and Vindication of the Church Founded by Our Lord Jesus Christ*. 1876. Facsimile ed. Amsterdam: Fredonia Books, 2004.

_____. "Jubilee Sermon Preached in the Baltimore Cathedral on Sunday, October 1, 1911". In *Retrospect*, 2:139–47.

Gower, Joseph F., and Richard M. Leliaert, eds. *The Brownson-Hecker Correspondence*. Notre Dame, Ind.: University of Notre Dame Press, 1979.

Grisez, Germain, and Russell Shaw. *Personal Vocation: God Calls Everyone by Name*. Huntington, Ind.: Our Sunday Visitor Publishing Division, 2003.

Herberg, Will. *Protestant, Catholic, Jew*. New York: Doubleday, 1955.

_____. "Religion and Culture in Present-Day America". In *Roman Catholicism and the American Way of Life*, edited by Thomas T. McAvoy, C.S.C., 4–19. Notre Dame, Ind.: University of Notre Dame Press, 1960.

Ireland, John, "Archbishop John Ireland: America in France". In *Readings in Church History*, edited by Coleman J. Barry, O.S.B. Westminster, Md.: Christian Classics, 1985.

John Paul II (pope). *Christifideles laici*. In *The Post-Synodal Apostlic Exhortations of John Paul II*, edited by J. Michael Miller, C.S.B. Huntington, Ind.: Our Sunday Visitor, 1998.

_____. *Ex corde Ecclesiae*. Falls Church, Va.: The Cardinal Newman Society, 1990.

Kantowicz, Edward R. "The Beginning and the End of an Era: George William Mundelein and John Patrick Cody in Chicago". In *Patterns of Episcopal Leadership*, by Gerald P. Fogarty, 202–15. New York: Macmillan, 1989.

Kauffman, Christopher J. *Faith and Fraternalism: The History of the Knights of Columbus, 1882–1982*. New York: Harper and Row, 1982.

_____. *Tradition and Transformation in Catholic Culture: The Priests of Saint Sulpice in the United States from 1791 to the Present*. New York: Macmillan, 1988.

Kelly, George A. *The Battle for the American Church*. Garden City, N.Y.: Image Books, 1981.

Ker, Ian. *John Henry Newman*. New York: Oxford University Press, 1988.

Lawler, Philip F. *The Faithful Departed: The Collapse of Boston's Catholic Culture*. New York: Encounter Books, 2008.

Leo XIII (pope). *Testem benevolentiae*, January 22, 1899. In Henry Denziger, *The Sources of Catholic Dogma*, trans. Roy J. Deferrari. St. Louis: B. Herder, 1957.

Maritain, Jacques. *The Peasant of the Garonne*. New York: Macmillan Paperbacks, 1969.

Marlin, George J. *The American Catholic Voter: 200 Years of Political Impact*. South Bend, Ind.: St. Augustine's Press, 2004.

Massa, Mark S., S.J. *The American Catholic Revolution: How the '60s Changed the Church Forever*. New York: Oxford University Press, 2010.

McAvoy, Thomas T., C.S.C., ed. *Roman Catholicism and the American Way of Life*. Notre Dame, Ind.: University of Notre Dame Press, 1960.

McBrien, Richard P. *The Remaking of the Church*. New York: Harper and Row, 1973.

McGreevy, John T. *Catholicism and American Freedom*. New York: Norton, 2003.

Morris, Charles R. *American Catholic: The Saints and Sinners Who Built America's Most Powerful Church*. New York: Times Books, 1997.

Murray, John Courtney, S.J. *We Hold These Truths: Catholic Reflections on the American Proposition*. New York: Sheed and Ward, 1960.

National Review Board. "A Report on the Crisis in the Catholic Church". *Origins*, March 11, 2–4.

O'Brien, David J. *Isaac Hecker: An American Catholic*. New York: Paulist Press, 1992.

_____. *Public Catholicism*. New York: Macmillan, 1989.

O'Connell, Marvin R. *Critics on Trial: An Introduction to the Catholic Modernist Crisis*. Washington, D.C.: Catholic University of America Press, 1994.

_____. *John Ireland and the American Catholic Church*. St. Paul, Minn.: Minnesota Historical Society Press, 1988.

O'Connor, Edwin, *The Edge of Sadness*. Boston: Little, Brown, 1961.

O'Connor, Flannery. Letter to Sister Mariella Gable, May 4, 1963. In *Flannery O'Connor: Collected Works*. New York: Library of America, 1988.

O'Connor, Thomas H. *Boston Catholics: A History of the Church and Its People*. Boston: Northeastern University Press, 1998.

O'Toole, James M. "The Name That Stood for Rome: William O'Connell and the Modern Episcopal Style". In *Patterns of Episcopal Leadership*, by Gerald P. Fogarty, 171–84. New York: Macmillan, 1989.

Percy, Walker. *Love in the Ruins*. New York: Avon Books, 1978.

Powers, J. F. "Prince of Darkness". In *Prince of Darkness, and Other Stories*. Garden City, N.Y.: Image Books, 1958.

_____. *Wheat That Springeth Green*. New York: Alfred A. Knopf, 1988.

Prendergast, William B. *The Catholic Voter in American Politics: The Passing of the Democratic Monolith*. Washington, D.C.: Georgetown University Press, 1999.

Reeves, Thomas C. *America's Bishop: The Life and Times of Fulton J. Sheen*. San Francisco: Encounter Books, 2001.

Rice, Charles E. *What Happened to Notre Dame?* South Bend, Ind.: St. Augustine's Press, 2009.

Robinson, Henry Morton. *The Cardinal*. New York: Simon and Schuster, 1950.

Santayana, George. *Character and Opinion in the United States.* London: Constable, 1924.

Scott, David, and Mike Aquilina, eds. *Weapons of the Spirit: Selected Writings of Father John Hugo.* Huntington, Ind.: Our Sunday Visitor Publishing Division, 1997.

Shaw, Russell. *Nothing to Hide: Secrecy, Communication and Communion in the Catholic Church.* San Francisco: Ignatius Press, 2008.

_____. *To Hunt, To Shoot, To Entertain: Clericalism and the Catholic Laity.* San Francisco: Ignatius Press, 1993.

Smith, Christian. *Soul Searching: The Religious and Spiritual Lives of American Teenagers.* With Melinda Lundquist Denton. New York: Oxford University Press, 2005.

Steinfels, Peter. *A People Adrift.* New York: Simon and Schuster, 2003.

Taylor, Charles. *A Secular Age.* Cambridge, Mass.: Harvard University Press, 2007.

Tocqueville, Alexis de. *Democracy in America.* Translated by Gerald Bevan. London: Penguin Books, 2003.

Varacalli, Joseph A. *Bright Promise, Failed Community: Catholics and the American Public Order.* Lanham, Md.: Lexington Books, 2000.

_____. *The Catholic Experience in America.* Westport, Conn.: Greenwood Press, 2006.

Vatican II. Pastoral Constitution on the Church in the Modern World, *Gaudium et spes,* 1965.

Whitehead, Kenneth D. *The Renewed Church: The Second Vatican Council's Enduring Teaching about the Church.* Ave Maria, Fla.: Sapientia Press, 2009.

Woodward, Kenneth L. "Memories of a Catholic Boyhood". *First Things,* April 2011.

INDEX

abortions, 134, 141–43, 149–50, 152, 157–58
academic freedom, 164–65
adoptions and gay couples, 204
Alberigo, Giuseppe, 114
Alcott, Bronson, 26
Allen, John, 175, 199–200
America (Jesuit weekly), 125
The American Catholic Revolution (Massa), 129
American Catholics and the Intellectual Life (Ellis), 98–99, 101, 104
American Freedom and Catholic Power (Blanshard), 65
Americanism, condemnation of, 42–51
Americanization of Catholic Church, 1–9, 13, 16, 62, 70
American Way of Life, 120–21
Anglo-Catholics, 183, 197
anti-Catholicism, 25, 34, 37–41, 65, 72–80, 99, 105, 119, 137
anti-communism, 89–92
Appleby, R. Scott, 51, 55
Aspirations of Nature (Hecker), 29
Associated Press polls, 184
atomic bombing of Hiroshima and Nagasaki, 88–89
The Awful Disclosures of Maria Monk (1835), 37

Baltimore Diocese, 35
Baltimore Sun, 44
baptisms, 22, 176, 182
Baxter, Michael, 11
Benedict XVI (pope), 11, 128–29, 145, 156–57, 195, 214. *See also* Ratzinger, Joseph
Benestad, J. Brian, 200–201
Benigni, Umberto, 54
Berger, Peter, 122
Bernanos, Georges, 79
Bernardin, Joseph L., 149–51
Biden, Joseph, 142
birth control, 7, 96, 125–27, 154–55, 203–4
Black, Hugo, 65
Blanshard, Paul, 65
Blondel, Maurice, 52
Bok, Sissela, 170, 170n60, 199n25
Boston Archdiocese, 173–75
Boston Quarterly Review, 26
A Brief History of Vatican II (Alberigo), 114
Brownson, Henry F., 80
Brownson, Orestes, 3–4, 25–34, 42, 56–57, 206
Brownson's Quarterly Review, 28, 30
Buonaiuti, Ernesto, 52
Burke, Margaret Gibbons, 18
Burleigh, Michael, 89n35